HIDDEN
HISTORY
of
EXETER

HIDDEN
HISTORY
of
EXETER

Barbara Rimkunas

THE
History
PRESS

Published by The History Press
Charleston, SC 29403
www.historypress.net

First published 2014

Manufactured in the United States

ISBN 978.1.62619.731.2

Library of Congress Control Number: 2014952377

Notice: The information in this book is true and complete to the best of our knowledge. It is offered without guarantee on the part of the author or The History Press. The author and The History Press disclaim all liability in connection with the use of this book.

Contents

Acknowledgements

This book would have been utterly impossible without the consistent help of my co-worker, Laura Martin. Laura reads and reviews each column I write for the *Exeter News-Letter* and cleans up my wild punctuation. We frequently run the pieces past Pam Gjettum, who volunteers for the Exeter Historical Society both as a researcher and member of the board of trustees. Her observations can send a particular story into an entirely different direction from where it was originally headed.

I depended on the advice of my brother, Tony Rimkunas, in choosing which articles to include in this collection. He has the advantage of not living in Exeter and is therefore a neutral party. Also, he's willing to read through hundreds of old newspaper columns without wanting to throw himself off a cliff.

The bulk of this work was researched at the Exeter Historical Society, and the photographs that accompany the chapters are from the archives unless otherwise noted.

Introduction

What is a "hidden history"? Is it a story that cannot be found or something hiding in plain sight? In the years I've been working at the Exeter Historical Society, I've come to discover that there are many perspectives with which to view events. A child's memory of an event will be quite different from an adult's—even when both were there. And some things seem to disappear from our collective memory. Why is that?

In 2013, the town of Exeter celebrated its 375th anniversary. As part of this, I was asked to do a presentation of the town's history. The essence of the work of a local historian is being asked to present 375 years of complex history in under ninety minutes. Sure, if I could stick to the bare bones and tell only a fragment of what has occurred here, I might be able to pull it off. I had to present a framework of Exeter, tell only the basic history—there could be no rambling on about fraternal organizations or early swine regulations. The slides that accompanied the talk had to be carefully chosen from our collections. There are thousands of photographs and images in the archives, but I needed to limit it to fewer than one hundred.

On the chosen night, we assembled in the Exeter Town Hall—the same place, I reminded everyone, where Abraham Lincoln spoke on a similar evening in 1860. As the talk progressed, it seemed to settle on a steady parade of, well, parade photos. We like to celebrate in Exeter, and this seems to be our chosen method (we also like fireworks, but they don't photograph as well, so they were left out of the public presentation).

To illustrate the coming of World War II, I included a photograph of Selective Service registration. The draft began a full year before Pearl Harbor, and I've always thought that the photograph of young Exeter men nervously waiting to register for military service had a spooky quality to it—their lives about to be interrupted with experiences beyond their own control. I lingered on the photo for a few moments to let that sink in. When I came out of my own momentary history spell, the audience was responding with odd murmuring and slight chuckles—a reaction that was quite unexpected. While absorbed in the scene, it hadn't missed anyone's notice (except perhaps mine) that we were in the same room where the young men were assembled in 1940, and it was further noticed with some delight—or perhaps horror—that the wooden settees in the photo were the exact same ones they were uncomfortably sitting on at that moment, broken slats and all. "Probably the same damn chairs used when Lincoln was here," someone later noted.

The missing bits of history, then, are usually the ones we cannot fit into the limited space of our usual storytelling. Since 2005, our local newspaper, the *Exeter News-Letter*, has provided space for the Exeter Historical Society to present bits and pieces of the town's history. Often, we celebrate anniversaries of organizations, businesses and events. Thank goodness there is interest in our historical landscape! If we didn't wonder about things like how long the bowling alley has been on Columbus Street, we might lose our history. Catching the things that are almost forgotten is the focus of this collection. This book begins with Reverend John Wheelwright and his followers, who founded the town. Wheelwright had to cobble together a governmental structure. Since those early days, townsfolk have coped with disease, dangerous livelihoods, superstitions, immigrant arrivals, crime and intrusive national events. We don't always get a chance to examine these topics within the usual framework of town elections and tax appropriations. The story behind the story—or, more correctly, the story beneath the story—often provides us with better context for why something may have occurred. What follows is an assortment of columns originally published in the *Exeter News-Letter* that best presents some of the hidden history of Exeter, New Hampshire.

PART I

Origins

As a town, Exeter has existed since 1638, making it old for America but only oldish for New England. There are plenty of other towns that were founded before 1638. Of course, if we could peek into the decades and centuries before 1638, there would be many more tales to tell. People have lived on the banks of the Squamscott River for perhaps thousands of years, and I, for one, would like nothing better than to slip into a time machine, travel back about four hundred years and hear the earliest history of our town. Generations of families who lived here probably had thousands of stories about troublesome children, bickering spouses, feckless leaders and terrifying creatures, all wrapped around the riverbanks that all of us—regardless of era—would recognize.

It's likely that different waves of people settled here just as they would after the Europeans' arrival. Each new food ways or clothing style left an impression on the ether that surrounds the town. Alas, in written form, we can only begin with the arrival of Reverend John Wheelwright and his small band of followers, who were stubborn enough to be convinced that they, and not the esteemed leaders of the Massachusetts Bay Colony, knew the clear path to heaven. The Wheelwright Deed is our liminal moment when two voices of storytelling met. The Englishmen signed the note with words, while Squamscott sagamore Wehenownowit and his comrade fixed their own images to the paper. We can, however, feel the pulsing of our earliest residents while we read the written history of the European arrival.

JOHN WHEELWRIGHT AND HIS CHURCH

Standing prominently in the center of Exeter's downtown is a majestic New England church. The Congregational Church of Exeter can trace its roots back to the original settlement of the town in 1638—indeed, the history of both the church and the town are inextricably linked.

Early in the seventeenth century, the Church of England was dealing with a protest movement (of sorts) among its members. Everyone agreed that the church needed to be clearly distinct from the Roman Catholic Church, but some also felt that it should completely reject any trappings of latent Catholicism that still lingered. These reformers, led by such men as John Cotton, referred to themselves as Puritans because of their desire to "purify" the church as it existed. Their resistance to such things as vestments, church hierarchy and their reliance on scriptural authority led to persecution by church authorities. By the 1620s, many Puritans had decided that they might do better if they went somewhere else. Some went to Holland but found the culture too different for their tastes. After that experiment, a decision was made to move entire families to the American wilderness during a period known as the Great Migration. During the time from 1629 to 1642, there was a rush of devout English immigrants leaving for Massachusetts Bay Colony.

What could go wrong? Here the Puritans could practice their religion with little oversight from the mother church back in England. It was never anticipated that the New England Puritans might begin to bicker among themselves, but that is just what happened. Before they had even left England's shores, there was disagreement over the covenant of works and the covenant of grace. How does one achieve salvation? They all agreed that a person must be able to relate a conversion experience to become a full member of the church—and therefore the elect—but how did one achieve this? Did a life of obedience and devout living, with material success, reflect that one was preordained for life-everlasting? Or could one ignore the strict societal rules and seek the truth through direct study of the scriptures and the intervening grace of God? It was a theological question that still sparks debate today.

Coming down on the side of grace was a small group of dissenters, including Anne Hutchinson and her brother-in-law, Reverend John Wheelwright. Accused of being "antinomian," or "against the laws,"

The Congregational Church of Exeter, circa 1890.

Reverend John Wheelwright (circa 1592–1679).

both were brought up before the legal system in Boston and expelled from the Massachusetts Bay Colony. Hutchinson chose to settle in Rhode Island, where Roger Williams had created a safe haven for religious dissent. Wheelwright, for reasons that he alone knew, decided to settle in

Monument dedicated to the original church building in Exeter, located on Salem Street.

the ungoverned wilderness of New Hampshire, at a spot along the falls of the Squamscott River.

Arriving in the fall of 1637, he wintered with one of the few Europeans living in the area, Edward Hilton, and set out the following March for the place that would be called "Exeter." His wife, children and many of his like-minded parishioners followed within a few months. By April, he had made an agreement with the local natives and began the process of creating a town.

The first meetinghouse was built on the western side of the river on Wheelwright's land. There is no trace of this building today, but there is a monument on Salem Street just before the railroad tracks to mark the site. The building must have been crude, as it was replaced in 1650. By then, Wheelwright had moved on to Wells, Maine, after Exeter fell under the governance of the Massachusetts Bay Colony. The town center drifted closer to the falls, where the water was used for sawmills and commerce. The church moved to the downtown to accommodate the population.

The current building is actually the fifth structure traced to Wheelwright's original congregation. Completed in 1799, it was designed and erected by Ebenezer Clifford and Bradbury Johnson, both of Exeter. Used for years as both church and meeting hall for the town, it was the center of town affairs and even housed the town bell.

FOUNDING DOCUMENTS OF EXETER

Americans are familiar with the founding documents of our nation, namely the Declaration of Independence and the Constitution. In Exeter, many of us are less familiar with the founding documents of our town: the Wheelwright Deed and the Exeter Combination.

When Reverend John Wheelwright arrived at the falls of the Squamscott River in March 1638, he was an unlikely pioneer. A bookish minister from Lincolnshire, England, he'd run afoul of both the Church of England and the strict Puritans of Massachusetts Bay Colony. After being banished from Massachusetts for teachings that appeared both heretical and seditious to the authorities, he decided to settle in the wilds of New Hampshire. Exeter was a perfect location, both because the waterfalls on the river provided an economic boost and because the area had never been claimed by Massachusetts. To ensure that he had clear rights to the land, Wheelwright made an agreement with Wehenownowit, the sagamore of the local Squamscott Indian tribe. Wheelwright and his followers were granted the land, and the Squamscotts retained all

Exeter's Wheelwright Deed, signed on April 3, 1638.

their planted fields and hunting and fishing rights. The Squamscotts were seasonal residents, preferring to head inland during the winter.

The deed, signed on April 3, 1638, granted the land to Wheelwright and five other men to be held in common. Once the town was more organized, land would be allocated to various families by the group. Wehenownowit and another member of the tribe—identified only as "James" on the deed—signed the document with pictographs of themselves. Wehenownowit is seen with a raised tomahawk. It is not known how much the two men understood what the deed was about, but there were few difficulties between the natives and Englishmen during the years they all cohabitated on the land. Only minor skirmishes involving loose pigs are recorded in the town records.

There were actually two deeds signed on April 3. The first deed is owned by the Exeter Historical Society and is kept secure in the collections. The second one, now missing, extended the southern boundary of the town past the Merrimack River. Wheelwright was uncertain where the actual border with Massachusetts was located and must have created two documents to cover all the possibilities. For many years, it was believed that Wheelwright Deed no. 2 was located at Phillips Exeter Academy; in fact, Albertus T. Dudley wrote about seeing the document in the 1930s. Current attempts to find it have been unsuccessful. Photocopies of this deed exist in the archives of both the Exeter Historical Society and the Phillips Exeter Academy, so the original must be out there somewhere.

Having secured rights to the land, Wheelwright and perhaps fewer than two hundred other people began to create a town. During the first year, survival would have been the most important goal, but with the arrival of spring, it became necessary to lay down some laws for the new community. New Hampshire was an odd colony in that it had no civil authority. The area had been granted to Captain John Mason in 1629, but by 1635, Mason had died without ever having set foot in the colony. The only other towns in the region—Dover, Strawberry Bank and Hampton—fell under the authority of the Massachusetts Bay Colony. Exeter's population decided in the spring of 1639 to send notice to the British authorities that the people intended to govern themselves by combining together. The document they created, called the Exeter Combination, pledged loyalty to the king and to God and clearly differentiated themselves from Massachusetts, even though they intended to use Massachusetts laws as their model. This document was signed on

The Exeter Combination, signed on July 4, 1639.

"Mon. 5th, d. 4th 1639," which, when decoded as the fifth month (with March as the first month of the year) and fourth day, means that it was signed on the Fourth of July in 1639—a rather happy coincidence with our later national holiday.

The Exeter Combination is contained within the early record books in the town vault. A comparison of handwriting indicates that both were written by John Wheelwright himself—although he spelled his name "Whelewright," which seems to be a misspelling by the man himself. In later documents, he spells his name "Wheelwright," as we are used to seeing it today. Exeter is lucky to have both of our founding documents still in existence and still located in the town. Most other New England towns lost their treasures long ago.

THE STRANGE JOURNEY OF THE WHEELWRIGHT DEED

When John Wheelwright arrived in Exeter in 1638, he gathered together a few local frontiersmen and drafted a legal deed to the land. The Squamscott tribe, led by the sagamore Wehenownowit, occupied the region primarily in the summertime. The agreement signed on April 3, 1638, protected the native hunting and fishing grounds and ensured the Englishmen would not interfere with any cleared land already under cultivation. It is this document that establishes the founding date of the town of Exeter.

It is odd, then, given the importance of this founding document, that it disappeared for nearly two hundred years. The next we hear of the Wheelwright Deed is a mention in the 1830 edition of *Belknap's History of New Hampshire*. The editor, John Farmer, was a noted historian and genealogist. In his comments, he mentioned that he possessed both of the early deeds of Exeter. How he acquired them was something of a mystery.

Exeter's historian, Charles Bell, obtained copies of both deeds for inclusion in his 1888 *History of Exeter, New Hampshire*. The second deed extended the boundary of the town to the Merrimack River. It was most likely produced a short time after the first deed to acknowledge the murkiness of the Massachusetts border. Wheelwright and many of his followers had been forced out of the Massachusetts Bay Colony over theological issues and would have wanted to ensure they were not living within its boundaries.

In 1911, the *Exeter News-Letter* quoted the *Boston Globe* in reporting that the two deeds were sold at auction. No buyer was listed, but the price was listed as $420. "This is probably more money than the sagamore got when he parted with the land to which he gave the white purchasers the title deed," noted the paper.

The 1911 buyer was most likely George F. Gunter, a millionaire candy maker and eccentric document collector from Chicago. It was from Gunter, or perhaps his estate, that the first Wheelwright Deed was most likely purchased by William Randolph Hearst in the 1920s for the astounding amount of $3,000. Hearst was known to collect all manner of antiquities, whether he was actually interested in their historical value or not.

During this entire period, Exeter historians, frustratingly, had no idea what had become of the actual deeds. There was word that the two deeds had been sold separately. A letter in the historical society collections from George Plimpton indicates that he purchased the second deed in 1936 at an auction house in New York and intended to donate it to Phillips Exeter Academy. What has become of this deed is unknown. There are photocopies, but the original is missing.

In 1938, the town's 300th anniversary celebration was planned with great pomp and fanfare. As this festive year was drawing to a close, Albertus T. Dudley received word that Hearst had suffered a slight downturn in his fortunes and was selling off some of his collections. Included in that collection was, unbelievably, the Wheelwright Deed of 1638.

The auction was set to take place in New York in two days' time. If the town was going to recover the document, it would have to act quickly. An emergency meeting of the historical society was hastily called. Dudley was dispatched to New York with a bidding limit of $2,500. His account of the auction ran in the paper the following week:

The Wheelwright Deed, to my dismay, provided the sensation of the evening. Only one rival bidder appeared, but he shouted his offers with an assurance that suggested that he was determined to have the deed, and that a few hundreds or thousands more or less meant nothing to him. As the bids mounted, at first by hundreds and then by fifties, the audience grew interested and some of them emotional. After $1,000,

Albertus T. Dudley, author and instructor at Phillips Exeter Academy, was instrumental in returning the Wheelwright Deed to Exeter. *Courtesy of Phillips Exeter Academy.*

I found myself calmly adding $50 to every bid of even hundred made by the unidentified person across the hall. His bark, however, proved worse than his bite. After a bid of $1,500, he fell silent, and my final $50 triumphed. The participation of the Exeter Historical Society in the Hearst sale from the day of the decision to the day of the purchase covered just 48 hours. On Monday night it decided to try its luck, on Wednesday night it owned the deed. Luck is the proper word to use.

The return of the Wheelwright Deed to Exeter may have also answered a few questions concerning its previous whereabouts. Upon examining it, Dudley noted:

Across our deed runs a blotting readable with the aid of a mirror as, "Deed from Stickney, Piscataquack, Exeter, 1638." It has been inferred from these words that John Farmer got the two deeds from one of the Stickneys in Concord. Two daughters of Rev. Woodbridge Odlin, of Exeter, married Stickneys. Woodbridge Odlin was the son and successor or Rev. John Odlin, who became pastor of the Exeter church in 1706. Recalling the importance of town ministers of that date, someone has ventured the guess that the holder of the deeds turned them over to the minister for safekeeping early in the 1700s, that they passed from John to Woodbridge and thence into the Stickney family from whom John Farmer obtained them. There is no evidence at all to support this theory, but as a purely imaginative reconstruction of history, it is as good as any other.

The Nuts and Bolts of Running a Town

The earliest years of Exeter's existence as a town must have been difficult. Following his expulsion from the Massachusetts Bay Colony, John Wheelwright found himself in the sparsely populated province of New Hampshire.

Wheelwright decided to stay and proposed creating a settlement at the falls of the Squamscott—a river and region so named for the seasonal native people who lived there when warm weather approached. A deal was brokered with the Squamscotts and two deeds drawn up granting the English rights of ownership to the land, while retaining the fishing, hunting and cultivation rights for the natives. The agreement seemed to suit everyone involved, and soon after, more Englishmen and their families arrived from Massachusetts to live in the new community.

New Hampshire, at that time, had no centralized government and for the first year of its existence, Exeter had no real government either. The people must have been far too busy building shelters, clearing land and getting in crops to worry about governance. By the next year, however, they had decided to get organized. The first order of business was to apportion the land. A year's worth of exploration had, no doubt, given them some familiarity with the landscape.

After setting aside the lands that had previously belonged to Edward Hilton, they began by giving each head of household a certain number of acres—somewhere between four and eighty, depending on need and social status—for cultivation. The meadows were apportioned among those who had cattle, and rules were set for the use of the forests and rivers.

Relations with the Squamscotts remained fairly calm, although the two groups must have marveled at their differing ways of procuring food. The natives came to Exeter in spring to fish in the river, gather berries and nuts and plant small crops such as corn and squash. Their meat (deer, pigeon, turkey and squirrel) could be found in abundance in the dense forests that surrounded the town. Pigeons were so plentiful that it was said a flock alight could block out the sun.

The English, on the other hand, insisted on bread, beef and pork— none of which could be gathered from the environment without a great deal of effort. Grain crops required cleared land and some type of mill to produce flour. Cattle and swine had to be tended and fed. Within a few years, the townspeople had assigned one person to tend the cattle each day. Cows were herded into the center of town each morning and taken to the woods to forage. In the evenings, they were returned to their homes.

Pigs, however, were more problematic. They weren't fed regular meals but rather were set loose each day to find their own food. As they rooted around for eatables, they sometimes destroyed local gardens. At a town meeting held in 1641, a local Exeter goodman was required to "allow the Indians one bushel of corne for ye labor wch was spent by ym in replantying of yt corne of yrs wch was spoyld by his swine." Loose pigs eventually led to strict laws regarding fences, and the job of "inspector of fences" became an important task.

Everyone in town was granted the right to fish on the river, provided that they did not infringe or destroy the native fishing weirs. In 1644, Christopher Lawson was granted the right to construct a weir, which was a structure for trapping fish, across the river. He was supposed to ensure that small boats and barks could still get through, but it must not have worked out because the next year, his grant was revoked and the rights of the river were extended back to all townsfolk.

Rights to the forests were also controlled by the town government. Within the first year, the central part of the village was largely deforested, and harvesting lumber was restricted to one half mile outside town. Since food production was low, lumber became the chief source of income for most residents. Most early records indicate that lumber finished into barrel staves and boards became the currency used in town instead of currency proper. Most of the local economy functioned on a barter system—including the payment of taxes, which were argued over as much as they are today.

In this manner of inventing rules as they were needed and regulating behavior regarding resources, the small community held together during the early years. When food was scarce, the council ordered a general search of all homes, and surplus food was divided among those who needed it—with the understanding that market price would be paid in exchange. The town thus avoided any of the "starving times" experienced in earlier settlements like Plymouth or Jamestown. Although the laws changed within several decades after the natives left and sawmills created a booming lumber industry, the town of Exeter began with seemingly humble gentlemen's agreements.

PART II

In Sickness and in Health

One's health history is a private matter. It's such a personal story that we reveal it only to those closest to us—unless, of course, we want to send our kids to camp. Then we're perfectly content to jot down every illness, vaccination and injury in order to get a few blessed weeks of peace and quiet. It's not a coincidence that medical practitioners' first inquiry into your health is called the "history." What follows is a brief snippet of Exeter's camp health form.

EXETER'S COUNTRY DOCTOR

When Dr. William G. Perry opened his office in 1847 in Exeter, he knew he had stiff competition. His father, also named Dr. William Perry, had been practicing medicine in town since 1814 and showed no signs of slowing down. The two men, designated "Old Dr. Perry" and "Young Dr. Perry," worked in town together for the next forty years, each serving his own patients but overlapping with great frequency.

"Old" Dr. Perry was not a native of Exeter. Born in 1788 in Norton, Massachusetts, he was a farmer's son. His father sent his two eldest sons to college but had to be coerced into doing the same for his third. It seems that he hoped young William would be the one to inherit the farm, but

Dr. William Perry (1788–1887).

the boy had other ideas. He headed to Union College in New York in 1807 but quickly decided to transfer to Harvard. On the trip home, he just happened to come upon a newfangled invention called a steamship that was making one of its first voyages down the Hudson River. Hopping aboard, William became one of the first people in America to ride on Robert Fulton's steamship.

In 1814, the same year Perry earned his MD from Harvard Medical School, the town of Exeter found itself in need of a new (or younger) physician. According the *Exeter News-Letter*, "About this time the people of Exeter were in want of a doctor. Some of the resident physicians were getting old and others lacked moral standing. A number of leading citizens wrote therefore to Dr. Warren, asking him to recommend a young man of promise to fill the vacancy. He at once selected Dr. Perry." With his mentor's approval, Perry set up his practice in February 1814. He would remain in practice until shortly before his death, at the age of ninety-eight, in 1887.

He soon proved himself to be an excellent physician and surgeon. In the early years of his practice, doctors performed operations without the benefit of anesthesia, which was frightening for both doctor and patient. The *News-Letter* noted of Perry, "He was not a rash practitioner, but he could be heroic when heroism was required. A grateful patient whose life was saved by amputation performed when the sufferer was apparently at the last extremity, remarked that his own pain was half forgotten—this was before chloroform was known—when he saw the big drops of sweat upon the surgeon's brow."

Doctors in the nineteenth century had to be made of tough stuff. They ministered to all people at all times of day or night, frequently for little or no payment. Perry wisely allowed himself to be vaccinated for smallpox even when he was advised that the disease was dying out. The advice didn't seem to apply to Exeter, as smallpox was still seen in the town: "He had abundance of work in this line, however. He attended numberless cases, sometimes burying with his own hand, those, who having died of the worst forms of the disease, had been abandoned by their terror-stricken friends." Such was the life of a village doctor.

Perry didn't confine himself to the study of medicine; he was also interested in the mechanics of the Industrial Revolution that came to town in the form of textile mills. Finding that the materials used for sizing cotton fabrics had to be imported from England, he devised a way to make the same type of starch from potatoes. His potato starch

Dr. Perry's trepanning kit, now in the collections of the Exeter Historical Society. Trepanning involved drilling burr holes into the skull to relieve headaches and other maladies.

mill on the Exeter River, just above the Great Bridge, operated for several decades, providing sizing for the mills in Lowell. Burned twice, the mill finally was put out of business by its own success. Dr. Perry had neglected to patent his discovery and lost customers when a competitor stole his process and set up his own potato starch mill.

Perry also dabbled in dentistry, carving replacement teeth from hippopotamus tusks. He filled cavities with such skill that local dentists remarked on their durability. It may have been his work in dentistry that led him to invent a simplified packing for the treatment of nosebleeds. Exeter's cotton mill provided the cotton wadding and strong thread that Perry used to pack the nose and later extract the wadding easily—without the use of damaging instruments. It was a simple solution for a difficult problem.

Dr. Perry continued to practice well into his eighties, performing three delicate hernia operations at the age of eighty-seven. His skill was such that the *News-Letter* noted that "a fourth time, when ninety-two, he was equally successful" with another hernia repair. It speaks well of his abilities that his patients harbored no reservations about letting him operate at such an advanced age.

At the time of his death, Perry was the oldest resident of the town of Exeter. "Few men will be more missed by all classes in our community than Dr. Perry," wrote the *News-Letter* in his obituary. "He was firm, and sometimes blunt even to roughness, with hypochondriacal patients or those he believed to be shamming. Toward real sufferers he was as gentle and sympathetic as a woman."

Quarantine

"Mom, I don't feel good." These are the most dreaded words a parent can hear first thing in the morning. The day's plans are shot, the school has to be notified, possibly a doctor's appointment has to be made and met, maybe a workplace has to be called, coverage found and ginger ale purchased. And always the potential threat looms that any other children in the family might become similarly afflicted within a few hours or days.

But except for a few rare cases, most of the time our main concern is the inconvenience. Kids get sick. Kids get better. We take for granted this usual progression of illness. A century ago, it wasn't quite so simple. For one thing, your child was likely to come home from school with something a lot worse than a stomach bug.

In 1900, the main childhood killers were infectious diseases such as scarlet fever, measles, diphtheria and whooping cough. All of these are highly contagious and would spread like a wildfire through classrooms. There were few vaccines and no effective treatments besides supportive care. The only tried-and-true way to prevent an epidemic was quarantine.

By the late 1880s, most states, including New Hampshire, had created a board of health. Regulations were enacted to close down ports if cholera were detected. Sanitation systems were improved to create cleaner streets and safer drinking water. And procedures were developed to make some illnesses "reportable." Local doctors were required to report and, if necessary, isolate any suspected cases of these illnesses.

The New Hampshire quarantine regulations from 1916 included the entire family of a sick child: "When a child is sick and suspected

Families with numerous children, such as the Graneys, pictured here in 1924, lived in trepidation of the restrictions that might be placed on the household if any of the children fell ill.

of having a contagious disease, other children in the family must not attend school until they produce a certificate from a respectable physician that there will be no danger of their communicating the disease to other pupils." A sign was placed on the family's house notifying everyone of the quarantine.

Usually, the father would escape to stay with a neighbor or other family member. His income was too important to lose because of a child's illness. But if both mother and father were employed—and in Exeter, many families had both parents working in the factories—quarantine created a financial hardship. The quarantine period was also very long. Today, if your child misses three days of school, it's considered unusual. The 1916 regulations required—at minimum—fifteen-day quarantine for measles and chicken pox and up to six weeks for scarlet fever and whooping cough. Why all the fuss? The following account from the *Exeter News-Letter* in January 1901 illustrates the difficulties and tragic outcomes that could happen. In this case, a teacher was the first to notice that one of her pupils had missed a number of days of class:

Miss Annie l. Davis, teacher of the Prospect hill primary noted her absence on Monday, and on inquiry of her scholars was told that she had the measles. Miss Davis promptly notified the school board, and that in turn the board of health. Dr. Nute made an immediate investigation Monday afternoon, having almost to force his way into the tenement. The girl, who the father declared was not very sick, was found by Dr. Nute to have not measles, but scarlet fever in pronounced form. He promptly quarantined the house, and gave the requisite instructions to its occupants, the men being unreasonable and hard to deal with. An hour later Dr. Nute had occasion to revisit the neighborhood, and found one of the children at a neighbor's and other violations of the quarantine. The board of health consequently invoked police aid.

The police placed a watch on the house and the entire neighborhood, but it was too late. The children next door quickly developed symptoms; their mother and older sister, who worked in the household of Phillips Exeter Academy professor John Kirtland, brought scarlet fever into the Kirtland home. The professor and his three sons developed the disease and became gravely ill. The two younger boys, aged ten months and three years, both died within a week of each other.

This particular episode took place before quarantine rules were well known among the general public, and it is of note that the violators were all recent Polish immigrants, who were unschooled in the newfangled rules of public health. The *News-Letter*'s article was meant as a cautionary tale, as the account of the events was preceded by a notice from the school board: "Even if new cases, already contracted, should develop, the teachers are on the watch for any symptoms of illness and will promptly report any case at its earliest stage."

Parents were under advisement that the children's health was being monitored. Sick children were reported, and children who missed school were investigated. As restrictive and financially devastating as quarantine could be, there was too much at stake.

INFLUENZA, 1918

"We should surely remain calm and not lose our good sense," advised the New Hampshire State Board of Health. "We must have confidence that our physicians and health officers, who have the real facts before them will give the situation every consideration." In the fall of 1918 the "situation" at hand was the arrival of a deadly worldwide influenza pandemic.

Individual cases of flu began to appear in Exeter in mid-September. School had been in session for only a few weeks, and the newspapers were still full of news of the war. Although many newspapers suppressed information regarding the flu to prevent panic, the *Exeter News-Letter* began to run stories directly related to the outbreak in the last weeks of the month. By that time, it would have been difficult to ignore the flu's grip on the town.

The 1918 influenza, sometimes called "Spanish influenza," was caused by a quick-spreading virus that could incapacitate its victims in hours. Some sufferers would slowly recover, while others would develop deadly pneumonia and die within days; the victims were generally people in the prime of life. Most flu epidemics preyed on the weakest members of society—the very old and the very young. This flu attacked adults between the ages of fifteen and fifty-five.

On September 27, the *News-Letter* reported, "The 'Spanish Influenza,' so-called, probably the grip in severe form after a cycle of comparative mildness, has gained a strong foothold in Exeter. Hundreds are affected by severe colds, grippe and too many by pneumonia. To list its victims is impracticable. They are of all classes and ages and in instances entire families are affected. Manufactories, stores, and schools have their victims." Exeter's public schools stopped all classes. The Ioka Theater was ordered closed by the board of health. The following week, most clubs, churches and public meetings were postponed due to the flu. Phillips Exeter Academy continued to hold classes, fearing that sending the students home might only spread the disease; nevertheless, the boys became sick, and the gymnasium had to be converted into an infirmary.

There was no need to panic, the public was counseled, even though the Cottage Hospital was quickly overwhelmed with critical patients and much of the staff became ill. Dr. William Day fell victim, and his slow recovery kept him from treating his patients. Not that there was much

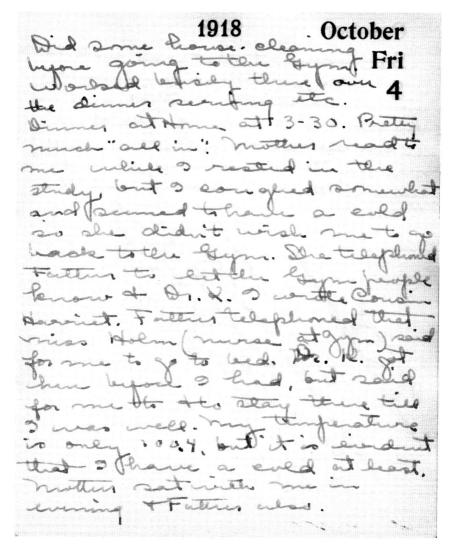

When influenza hit Exeter in 1918, young Helen Tufts volunteered to help nurse the ill students at Phillips Exeter Academy. As her diary demonstrates, she herself quickly became sick. Her recovery took several weeks.

that could be done for flu victims. Even today, there is little but supportive care that can be done for those suffering from influenza.

By the first week in October, the death toll had become a daily feature in the obituary columns. William Murray, the Boston postmaster, died. Democratic Congressional candidate Edward Cummings died. And

Robert Kent had just returned from the war and was due to take over management of the Exeter Manufacturing Company when he succumbed to the flu on November 24, 1918.

well-loved townspeople died: "Mr. Charles B. Edgerly, superintendent of lines for the Exeter & Hampton Electric Company, and Miss Marion I. Fogg, of Hampton Falls, long a clerk in its office were married here last Saturday by Rev. John W. Savage, of Seabrook. It was necessarily a simple wedding, the bride then being affected by the influenza. Her condition since failed and early in the week she was compelled to enter the hospital, where she died last night of pneumonia."

So many people died during the week of October 4 that the *News-Letter* headed an entire column, "Deaths from Pneumonia." Immigrants, like thirty-three-year-old Stanislaus Yankowskas, a shoe worker, died as quickly as wealthy highborn people. The Kent family, owners of the Exeter Manufacturing Company, lost their eldest son, Robert, who, like Yankowskas, was thirty-three years old. Robert Kent had been slated to take over management of the mill. His death left the job to his widowed mother, Adelaide.

No family in Exeter suffered as much as the Tewhill family of Garfield Street. A tightknit Irish family, the Tewhills lost three family members to the flu. At one point during the epidemic, there were five gravely ill people in the household, leaving the remaining two as caretakers. Stories such as this trickled in from all parts of the country. The death toll in Exeter was thought to be about twenty-five, but it would be higher if you counted those who died of pneumonia just before or just after the height of the epidemic.

After the terrible month of October, the town began a slow recovery. Schools reopened in the first week of November. The Exeter Public Library graciously provided amnesty for any overdue book fines for books checked out after September 21. Reports changed from obituary notices to those of recovery. "Chief [of police] Elvyn A. Bunker resumed his duties on Monday after a long sickness from the influenza," chirped the *News-Letter* on October 25. "We seem to be passing from out the shadow of the pestilence, and there is a marked decrease in the number of new cases. Many who have been seriously ill are now nearing recovery."

As hopeful rumors of a possible armistice in Europe began to surface in town, no news was received as joyfully in the tired town as this: "Miss Ellen Tewhill, who has been so seriously ill, on Tuesday walked from her Garfield Street home down town and back."

EXETER IN THE AGE OF POLIO

Under the headline of "Great Medical Victory," the *Exeter News-Letter* announced in April 1955, "A crowning achievement and a milestone in medical history came Tuesday with the announcement of success for the Salk polio vaccine." Within a week, the Rockingham County Medical Society was discussing plans to hold mass immunizations in the county. Time was of the essence; polio season typically occurred during the summer months. By late May, the first clinics were underway. "It is a tribute to the common senseness of adults that a vast majority of parents reasoned that the advantages of child inoculation far outweighed the over-publicized risks," commented the *News-Letter.*

Strangely, polio epidemics were fostered by improvements in sanitation and medical care. Transmitted by fecal-oral route, it was easily passed around among children. In earlier (and less hygienic) times, most children encountered the virus early in life. As the germ theory became better understood in the twentieth century, personal hygiene took a great leap forward simply by encouraging children to wash their hands before eating. By the early 1900s, most of the fecal-oral illnesses could be prevented by simply keeping clean. But oddly, this meant that there was little early exposure to the poliomyelitis virus.

The belief that sanitary methods would save the nation continued into the 1940s and '50s. Mothers were encouraged to give up breastfeeding in favor of clean, controllable bottle feeding. But bottle-fed babies do not receive their mother's immunities, making them vulnerable to pathogens like polio. Further reducing many children's natural immunity was the common practice of performing tonsillectomy procedures on children in the postwar period. Tonsils are the first line of defense against inhaled or swallowed foreign pathogens. In the 1950s, the connection between tonsillectomy operations and polio was noted, and it was recommended that the procedure not be done during the summer months, when polio outbreaks were common. It never occurred to anyone that perhaps relatively healthy tonsils should be left alone.

Even as researchers worked tirelessly to create a vaccine for the disease, polio cases increased dramatically in the post–World War II period. The peak of the epidemic was in 1952, when fifty-eight thousand cases were diagnosed in the United States.

Notices such as this one, which ran in the *Exeter News-Letter* in June 1950, were a common sight during the polio years.

Exeter and Rockingham County reported numerous cases of polio in the 1950s. Even though it was still statistically a small number of children who were affected, the fear of polio was profound. Parents were advised to keep children from getting exhausted or chilled. Many towns closed public swimming pools, although Exeter had none to close. Historian

Doris Kearns Goodwin, who grew up during the polio years in New York, recalled in her memoir, *Maybe Next Year:*

Lack of understanding about the spread of polio created a vacuum which parents and editorialists filled with a thousand admonitions: avoid crowded places where you may be sneezed or coughed upon; beware of contacts in trains, buses, or boats; keep children away from strangers; avoid swimming in cold water; don't sit around in wet clothes; don't play to the point of getting overtired; avoid public drinking fountains; avoid using one another's pencils, whistles, handkerchiefs, utensils, food; burn or bury garbage not tightly covered; wash your hands before eating; call your doctor immediately if you've got a stiff neck, upset stomach, headache, sore throat, or unexplained fever.

Local cases were publicized by the March of Dimes campaigns to help encourage donations. President Franklin Roosevelt's National Foundation for Infantile Paralysis helped cover the staggering costs that families faced when a member needed round-the-clock care and rehabilitation. Mild cases were treated at Exeter Hospital; those requiring iron lung treatments were sent to the Children's Hospital in Boston or Elliot Hospital in Manchester. Long-term rehabilitation was done at New Hampshire's Crotched Mountain Rehabilitation Center, which was built in 1950. The photos and news stories did a great deal to increase donations, but they also served as a source for a steady stream of parental fear in a time when there was already plenty to fear. If the increasingly frightening Cold War and atom bomb weren't enough, polio could strike your child during the hot summer months and disable him or her for life. Was it any wonder, then, that when a viable vaccination was created, parents were quick to sign up their children?

The first mass vaccination in Exeter occurred in May 1955. Limited to children in the first and second grade, the clinic was a cooperative effort. The *Exeter News-Letter* reported:

Upon arrival at the gym, accompanied by their teachers, the children were given basic medical tests by volunteer nurses and they then stood attentively in line while the classmate ahead was given the quick but nonetheless skillful and painstaking treatment by Dr. Nolan and Dr. Tuthill. Teaming up with the two doctors were Mrs. Dean J. Thorp, Jr., R.N., and Lieutenant Commander Angelica Vetullo of the Portsmouth

Naval Hospital. Seven naval corpsmen provided valuable assistance by measuring the serum for the individual doses.

There were a few more years of dangerous outbreaks. Phillips Exeter Academy delayed opening in 1955—the first year of the polio vaccine—because of the fear of outbreaks among students arriving from Massachusetts. In 1956, vaccination clinics were opened up for all children under the age of fifteen, as well as pregnant women. By 1957, teenagers and adults were encouraged to get vaccinated. The development and widespread use of the Sabin oral vaccine in 1962 further slashed national polio rates. In 1964, only 121 cases of polio were reported in the entire United States. Summers filled with the fear of a dreaded disease were a thing of the past.

PART III
Conflicts and Heroes

E xeter's slave history is a complicated one. There were people enslaved in town, just as there were people enslaved across the rest of New Hampshire. Although the practice died out after the American Revolution, it was still technically legal until the passage of the Thirteenth Amendment in 1865. Exeter's population before the Civil War was more racially diverse than it is today, and yet there was no full embrace of the abolitionist movement in town. Slavery was viewed as a necessary evil confined to a particular part of the nation. Our town, with an enormous textile mill on the waterfall, depended on slave labor to produce the cotton, which was then woven into fabric by white hands running the machinery. Black workers were unable to find work in Exeter's mill. Yet we tend to avoid this conflict when we talk about our town. There were men from Exeter who went west to fight for Texan independence and, later, defended it as part of the slaveholding United States. And there were also men and women willing to fight and work toward a United States free of slavery.

JOSEPH MARCH CHADWICK AND THE MASSACRE AT GOLIAD

In 1936, Texas commemorated one hundred years of independence from Mexico by erecting a monument to the officers and soldiers who fell at Goliad. Among the names carved into the pink granite is that of Exeter native Joseph March Chadwick. Only twenty-four when he was executed by the forces of Santa Anna, Chadwick was participating in an adventure far, far from home.

Chadwick was born in Frankfort, Maine, in 1812 to Exeter parents Susan Coffin March and Colonel Peter Chadwick. The family moved back to Exeter shortly after Joseph's birth, so we can probably still consider him a native of the town. At the age of ten, he entered Phillips Exeter Academy and completed a course of study that prepared him well for his entrance, in 1829, to West Point. Poor health made him resign after only two years of study, but the USMA trained him well in draftsmanship and military discipline.

At the tender age of nineteen, Chadwick headed west to St. Louis. He seems to have been the type of person who needed to be in the open air. A short stint in the land office found him again in a state of indisposition. He joined Colonel Dodge on a hazardous expedition into Pawnee country, where he befriended artist George Caitlin. Caitlin would become internationally famous for his portraits of Native Americans. He well remembered Joseph Chadwick. The expedition was struck by an outbreak of cholera, and Caitlin suffered tremendously. His friend Chadwick was always at his side, nursing him along and helping him to slowly recover. Two years after the expedition, the two men met again in St. Louis, and Caitlin painted Chadwick's portrait. He was pleased with the likeness and wrote that he had caught "all the fire and all the game look" of the young man. Chadwick sent the portrait off to his mother in Exeter. He was headed farther west on a new adventure in Texas.

After a long struggle, Mexico gained its independence from Spain in 1821. Within a decade, English-speaking Americans had begun to settle in the northern portion of the country. They brought with them a dislike of Mexico's state-sponsored Roman Catholic religion and a preference for slave labor. By 1834, there were an estimated thirty-five thousand English speakers, including five thousand slaves, living

Sketch of Joseph March Chadwick made by George Caitlin.

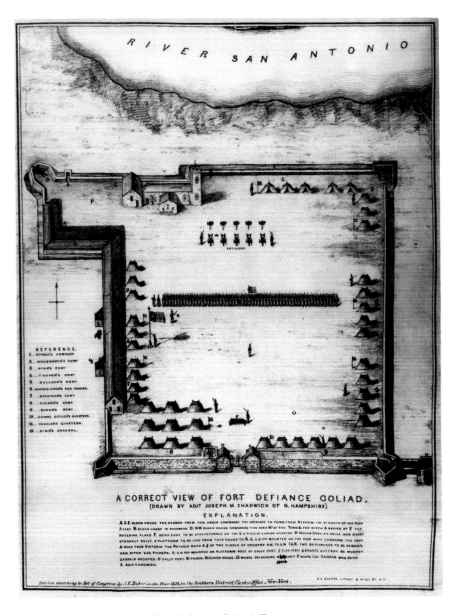

Joseph Chadwick's sketch of Fort Defiance, Goliad, Texas.

in the territory—numbers that far exceeded the Spanish speakers. Alarmed by the rapid rate of immigration, Mexico prohibited any further settlement by Americans.

Texans rose up in rebellion late in 1835. Chadwick joined the fray in early 1836 under the command of Colonel Fannin at Goliad. The *Exeter News-Letter* would later write of him, "On the 17th of January, when the Texan flag of Independence was unfurled, he was one of the number that run it up, paid it its first salute, and resolved, without fear or faltering, to march under and defend it."

The early battles in the war were dominated by Mexico. The Alamo fell on March 6, with Texan losses of more than two hundred men. Fannin is often criticized for not responding quicker to calls for help from the Alamo. He held back and, too late, realized that his own stronghold at Goliad was threatened. Marching his troops north toward Victoria, Fannin's men were surrounded in the desert by Mexican troops. On March 20, they surrendered to the Mexican forces and were marched back to Goliad. There, they signed papers of surrender, expecting to be treated as prisoners of war. But President Antonio Lopez de Santa Anna had recently passed a law that all foreigners under arms would be treated as pirates and executed. He was furious that the men were taken prisoner and ordered immediate execution. On the morning of March 27, 1836, the 342 prisoners were marched into the desert in three groups and shot. A few managed to escape, and for a time, there was some hope that Chadwick was among them. But in July, news reached Exeter that he was among the dead.

"Since the intelligence of the massacre of Fannin's detachment, at Goliad, was received, we have felt no little anxiety for a young gentleman, who was known to have been one of Fannin's staff, a short time before the surrender. The *St. Louis Bulletin* of July 1, removes all doubt upon the subject, and gives us the melancholy assurance that our friend has fallen." The obituary of Joseph Chadwick from St. Louis was a lengthy one.

He was a young man of great promise, not happily contained in classroom or office. The *Exeter News-Letter* summed up: "It is seldom, indeed, that a young man of the age of Mr. Chadwick, has seen so much of the world as he, been engaged in so much of enterprise and peril, formed so extensive an acquaintance, secured so many powerful and ardent friends, and attained and preserved a reputation so high, so pure and irreproachable. He died young, but will not soon be forgotten."

JOHN TOWLE AND THE MEXICAN-AMERICAN WAR

"Deaths: In this town, last evening, Mr. John Towle, age 26; he was a soldier in the Mexican War." So goes a simple obituary published in the *Exeter News-Letter* on January 8, 1849. Charles Bell's *History of the Town of Exeter* makes no mention of the Mexican-American War, and although he lists veterans for every other conflict, there are none listed for this one. President Polk's vision of "Manifest Destiny"—expansion of the nation from coast to coast—was seen by New Englanders as a backdoor way of introducing more slave states and disrupting the delicate balance of power. So it came as a surprise at the Exeter Historical Society to find that one of our residents had volunteered to serve.

Following the annexation of Texas in 1845, the United States tried to forge a deal with Mexico to buy California and the Southwest. The Mexican government, still seething over the unresolved boundary dispute with Texas, snubbed the offer. Polk sent troops to the Rio Grande to defend the boundary, and it wasn't long before shots were fired. War was declared in May 1846. The Americans won most of the early battles, easily taking California and New Mexico. A planned assault on Mexico City would require fresh troops, and a call was put out for volunteers in the spring of 1847.

Recruitment for a New England regiment was led by Franklin Pierce—a lawyer, former senator and militia officer with political ambitions. Pierce was a strong defender of the constitutional right of states to regulate slavery. This didn't always make him popular in the state, but his charm, good looks and patriotism were enough to help draw in recruits. We'll never know exactly what inspired a farm boy like John Towle to join up, but it was most likely a need for adventure. Even the recruiting advertisements in the *Exeter News-Letter* downplayed the danger: "Persons desirous of visiting Mexico, in the capacity of soldiers in the United States Army, may have an opportunity of enlisting at Portsmouth, Concord, Nashua or Manchester. The recruiting officers however, are very particular as to size, manners, and morals. They want men 5 feet 3 inches high, of *good character*, and *respectable standing.*" They were offered a twelve-dollar bounty, seven-dollars-per-month pay and "160 acres of land, somewhere, on being honorably discharged."

Chandler Potter's *Military History of New Hampshire* lists John Towle as a sergeant in Captain Stephen Woodman's Company C of the Ninth

The grave of John Towle (1823–1849) at the Winter Street Cemetery, Exeter, New Hampshire. Towle was the only soldier from Exeter to die during the Mexican-American War.

Regiment. He enlisted on April 1, 1847, in Dover. This is most likely why Exeter has never come across him in the official records. But he was from Exeter. His parents, Abraham and Mary Towle, were married in Exeter and lived here their entire lives. They had three sons—a baby, named John, died before his second birthday, and another son, Daniel, tragically drowned when he was seven. Their second John may have felt it was best to enlist a little farther away from home.

Company C sailed from Newport on May 21 aboard the *North Bend*, captained by Caleb Sprague of Barnstable. The journey was long and arduous, taking just over a month. Most of the soldiers suffered from seasickness, but worse ailments were waiting in Mexico. When they landed at Vera Cruz in June, the season of the dreaded *vomito* (yellow fever) was in full swing. Brigadier General Pierce managed to keep his soldiers relatively healthy by camping outside the city limits. His task was to march the troops 250 miles over land to Mexico City and reinforce the troops of General Winfield Scott. Like most wars of this time, disease took more lives than combat.

As the men marched, they died. The heat took a toll, as did dysentery, measles, influenza and malaria. Richard Bruce Winders commented in his book, *Mr. Polk's Army*, "The number of deaths was staggering: 110 out of every thousand participants died of disease, accident or wounds. The only other war that approaches this high rate of mortality is the Civil War, with its rate of 65 per thousand. To put this in perspective, out of a typical Mexican War regiment, more than one-tenth of its men did not survive their term of service." Towle was lucky to survive the march at all, let alone the battle. Mexico City fell in September. Pierce, who fell off his horse, was injured but endured through the battle and returned home to Concord the following January. Towle was able to reach Portsmouth and file for his military pension in August 1848. Eligible for eight dollars per month, he never collected. Pensions were paid every six months, and Towle died four months after filing.

THE QUESTION OF SLAVERY

Yes, there were slaves who lived in Exeter, New Hampshire. Contrary to what many of us learned in school, the New England states weren't all

NOTICE.

THE people of *colour* throughout the State are respectfully invited to appear at the residence of LONON DAILEY in Exeter, on Wednesday the 13th day of August next at 10 o'clock in the forenoon, for the purpose of forming a society beneficial to said people. The particular objects of the society will be made known at the time and place aforesaid.

Per order of LONON DAILEY.

RUFUS E. CUTLER, *Sec'y.*

N. B. An Oration will be pronounced at the Court-House on said day at 3 o'clock in the afternoon.

Exeter, July 22, 1817.

Notice placed in the *Exeter Watchman* in July 1817 by Exeter townsmen Lonon Daily and Rufus Cutler. The results of the meeting are unknown, as no records have ever surfaced.

abolitionist strongholds. There may not have been large plantations with hundreds of enslaved people, but there were slaves here nonetheless.

There were many levels of servitude in the colonial era. Apprentices and indentured servants served time without pay, but these arrangements had an endpoint and did not extend to one's offspring. Slavery kept a person in bondage for life, with little or no chance of escaping the system.

New England's enslaved people lived under different conditions from those held in the Southern states. Long winters in the North meant that there were months out of each year that could be very unproductive agriculturally. Instead, slaves in the North performed other types of labor. Tasks such as chopping firewood, hauling water, laundry, fishing and loading and unloading ships, as well as assisting artisan masters, were performed by enslaved people. The boring, repetitive work—working the machinery, pulling the printing press, hand weaving, cleaning, sweeping, gardening and even some farming—was done by people considered less valuable to society.

There was also an element of social status in having an enslaved person working in your home. Why hire a housekeeper or cook when you can raise your social standing by being able to afford someone you actually own? To those who were enslaved, of course, the system was horrid. Slaves had no rights. They had no right to themselves, they were not allowed to marry without consent, their children were owned by someone else at birth, they had no personal property and they could be bought or sold at will. It didn't matter that they were living in New England—slavery was slavery. It wasn't "better" just because it was in a northern colony.

In 1767, Exeter had fifty slaves living in town, spread among a number of owners. By the time of the Revolution, the census takers changed the category from "slaves" to "Negros slaves for life," leaving it an open question whether all people of color were enslaved or not. At that time, there were thirty-eight people listed in that group. By 1790, there were only two people listed as "slaves" in town. Did the Revolution eliminate slavery in New Hampshire? Here the question becomes a bit muddy.

The short answer is that New Hampshire forgot to outlaw slavery. Legally, that is. The Revolution ruined slavery in the state but never fully removed the system. Our state constitution, approved in 1783, states that "all men are born equal and independent"; it is mute on the legality of slavery, and the question was never challenged in court. A previous attempt, in 1779, by the black community of Portsmouth to petition for freedom was tabled in the legislature indefinitely. A later act, passed in 1857, specifying that "no person, because of decent, should be disqualified from becoming a citizen of the state," also didn't specify that slavery was illegal. By that time, however, there were no slaves listed in the U.S. Census for New Hampshire. Most people assumed that the practice was gone. Slavery was officially outlawed in New Hampshire with the passage of the Thirteenth Amendment to the U.S. Constitution in 1865.

Another question that frequently arises in relation to slavery in Exeter is whether the Underground Railroad operated in town. Although there are some local legends, there doesn't appear to be any actual evidence leading us to believe that fugitive slaves were hidden in town. There are a few houses that have hidden rooms in the layout, although these may simply be tricks of architecture used to conceal built-in bookshelves or utility access. The people who lived in the houses in the early part of the nineteenth century were not known to be abolitionists or Quakers. Of course, the Underground Railroad was a secret organization, so it can be difficult to find evidence of its existence. There are no accounts of fugitive slaves in Exeter and, as far as we can tell, no stories from successful runaways that mention Exeter as having been part of the trip.

Exeter after the Revolution attracted a number of former slaves, and at one time, the free black community was 4.0 percent of the town's population (2010 census data indicates a 0.6 percent African American population in Exeter). Considered trustworthy, though a lower social class, African Americans in Exeter found it difficult to compete in the economic market once white immigrants began arriving from Canada, Poland, Germany and Ireland. Mill owners refused to hire the descendants of former slaves, and the population gradually diminished over time.

ABOLITIONISM IN EXETER

On October 12, 1853, former Exeter congressman Amos Tuck organized a meeting of antislavery men from various political parties and united the group with a new name: the Republican Party. Exeter's claim to the founding of the Republican Party has been challenged over the years, but even if Tuck's meeting is only recognized as one of a few possible candidates, it still raises the question of Exeter's dedication to the abolitionist movement.

When the 1790 census was taken, there were still two enslaved people living in Exeter. The practice fell out of favor, even though the New Hampshire Constitution never actually prohibited its existence. Although New Englanders were more than willing to buy goods and products made by slaves, they weren't comfortable keeping slaves themselves.

With that said, it's hard to tell whether New Englanders were opposed to southerners keeping slaves. Before the Civil War was fought, most Americans still thought of themselves along regional, not national, lines. If the southern states wanted slavery, so be it. It wasn't illegal, according to the Constitution.

In 1834, slavery ceased to exist in Great Britain. Enslaved people were granted gradual emancipation through an apprentice system that lasted for nearly a decade, but the practice was outlawed for all intents and purposes. Emboldened by this, American abolitionists began to push for a similar ban. Unfortunately, that crusty old U.S. Constitution stood in the way. Without an amendment banning the practice, there was no way slavery would end.

That same year, the women of Exeter fired off a petition to the U.S. Senate and House of Representatives requesting that the practice of slavery be prohibited within the confines of Washington, D.C. They may not have been able to influence what happened in the individual states, but the capital city was federal land. Visiting dignitaries were often horrified to witness scenes of slave auctions upon arrival to Washington. The women of Exeter—representing all social groups and all the major churches in town—used the strongest possible language: "The undersigned, women of Exeter New Hampshire believing that slavery is a sin, and therefore 'a reproach to any people,' especially the free, enlightened and liberal government of which your honorable body form a part; and being grieved at its existence in the capital of our beloved country, the District over which you have exclusive jurisdiction, do unite our fervent, importunate petitions with the thousands already presented that you would immediately abolish Slavery in the District of Columbia, that henceforth, whoever breathes its air or touches its soil may be free."

They were part of a larger movement of northern abolitionists. So many petitions were delivered to Congress that in 1836 a committee finally instituted a rule that automatically tabled discussion and consideration of any more that might arrive. The existence of these petitions might lead one to believe that Exeter was a solidly abolitionist town. But another event, on August 11, 1836, highlights how contentious and divisive the issue really was.

The Methodist church, then located on Portsmouth Avenue, had agreed to host a fiery abolitionist speaker named Reverend Storrs. As the meeting began, the church was surrounded by an angry mob, which, according to the *Exeter News-Letter*, "interrupted the services—

Exeter's Methodist church, on Portsmouth Avenue, was the site of a mob attack on an abolitionist meeting in 1836.

stones were thrown—glass and window blinds broken—the fire engine brought out and made to play upon the building—until the Lecture was given up and the audience dispersed." Public opinion leaned toward the rioters' side. It wasn't so much the idea of abolition to which they objected; it was *abolitionists* that made them uncomfortable. What right did they have to agitate? One letter writer placed the blame for the event firmly on the organizers: "I think the injudicious conduct of the Abolitionists is making this great evil still greater, not only to the slave holder, but to the slaves themselves."

The divide in Exeter was similar to the divide everywhere in the North. Mark Sammons and Valerie Cunningham summed it up convincingly in *Black Portsmouth*: "There were gender issues at play too. White males typically assumed slavery was an aspect of business, finance, trade, and the economy. As a topic for debate, men fell squarely in the male domain. Women and abolitionists viewed slavery as a moral evil, an outlook that brought the debate within what was called the women's sphere. Among whites, women became advocates of abolition."

The ladies' petition failed to end slavery in Washington, D.C. In 1850, after a great deal of debate and outright fighting, President Millard

Fillmore reluctantly signed a compromise bill that eliminated slave trading, but not slave ownership, in the capital. It would take a much bloodier event, the Civil War, to eliminate the practice completely.

AMOS TUCK AND ABRAHAM LINCOLN

When Abraham Lincoln arrived in Washington in 1847 to start his sole term in the House of Representatives, the only seat left in the great hall was near the back. Next to him sat Amos Tuck of Exeter, New Hampshire. Tuck and Lincoln were of different political parties and often voted on opposite sides of issues, but the two men formed a friendship. Twelve years later, Tuck's newly formed Republican Party would catapult Lincoln onto the national stage.

Amos Tuck was born in Parsonsfield, Maine, in 1810. His family was originally from Hampton, New Hampshire, but hoped to find better farmland in Maine. Tuck himself never cared for farming and, from an early age, longed to pursue a more educated vocation. In his autobiographical sketch, published in serial form in the *Exeter News-Letter* in 1920, he recalled that "little besides the monotony of farm work entered into my life till 16 or 17 years of age." He begged his father to send him to a tuition school, but the family finances prohibited such expenditure. For the next decade, Tuck tried again and again to obtain the college education he desired. He taught school, worked in the fields and tutored students to earn money. Offered scholarships on several occasions, he turned them down because all required him to join the ministry. Tuck had set his sights on becoming a lawyer. His father never seemed to understand his son's ambition and regularly discouraged him from further education—the time and expense it would require would only prevent him from earning an honest living.

Likewise, Abraham Lincoln's father never understood his son's desire for knowledge. Lincoln grew to be a powerful, strong young man, and yet he seemed to waste his physical attributes, spending his time reading instead of plowing. Like Tuck, once he reached his late teens, he no longer felt obliged to his father. It was perhaps these early experiences that brought the two men together when they met in Congress.

The Honorable Amos Tuck (1810–1879).

Tuck was finally able to attend and graduate from Dartmouth College and passed the New Hampshire bar in 1838. He was quickly drawn into politics, becoming a member of the Democratic Party in New Hampshire. But by the 1840s, he had become disillusioned with the party over the question of slavery. The annexation of Texas, with its subsequent extension of slavery into new territory, was looming.

Tuck wasn't a supporter of slavery, but like most New Englanders, he was willing to tolerate it where it already existed. Texas would nearly double the slaveholding territory in the United States, and the question of whether slavery should be extended in other western territories was unresolved.

The Democratic Party in New Hampshire was in the death grip of proslavery men like Franklin Pierce. It prompted Tuck to hold a meeting in February 1845 in the vestry of the First Parish Church in Exeter to oppose the party platform. The meeting was held on Saturday, February 22. The group, calling itself "Independent Democrats," wrote a series of resolutions opposing the expansion of slavery into the territories and the annexation of Texas in particular. John P. Hale was nominated as candidate for the U.S. Senate and surprised everyone by winning the election. He would be the sole antislavery voice in the Senate for the next two years.

Tuck ran for Congress the following year, winning the election and finding himself seated next to Lincoln, another junior congressman. Lincoln's views on slavery were still evolving when the two men served together, but over the course of the next few years, he began to drift away from the Whig Party platform. Amos Tuck became more antislavery in his beliefs and, in March 1854, held a meeting in Exeter at the Squamscott House that would create the Republican Party that Lincoln would later embrace.

The friendship continued even after both left Congress. It was at Tuck's suggestion that Robert Lincoln, having failed his Harvard entrance exams, enrolled at Phillips Exeter Academy in 1859 for a year of hard cramming. When Lincoln visited Exeter in the spring of 1860, Tuck was sorry to have missed him. He wrote to Lincoln shortly afterward, "I very much regretted that I was absent when you were at Exeter, and was sorry you did not call upon my family, even in my absence." Although we do not know exactly where Abraham Lincoln stayed while in Exeter, we can be fairly certain that he did not stay at the home of Amos Tuck. In spite of this, there is a plaque on the house at 89 Front Street that notes that Lincoln *did* stay there. Given the close friendship between the two men, it would be more accurate if it read, "Abraham Lincoln should have slept here."

THE CIVIL WAR BEGINS

When Abraham Lincoln won the presidential election in November 1860, there was celebrating in the streets of Exeter. The *Exeter News-Letter* reported, "The streets were filled with the multitude of men, women and children. The wide awakes, in uniform and with torches blazing marched through the principal streets, throwing off fireworks and giving hearty cheers as they passed along preceded by the Exeter Cornet Band, whose excellent music was frequently praised by the spectators. The bells of the several churches were ringing during the evening until 10 o'clock."

But the celebrations were tempered within a week with threats of secession from South Carolina and Georgia. In Exeter, as in other parts of the country, the sword rattling seemed premature and uncalled for. "They know, or they ought to know, that Mr. Lincoln will not interfere with slavery in the States where it is established by law," commented the *News-Letter* editor. The Constitution allowed slavery, and as far as most Exeter citizens were concerned, it could continue to exist in those states that allowed it. Lincoln was opposed to the spread of slavery in the western territories. Why should his opposition to slavery in, say, Kansas, be cause for breaking up the Union?

As the New Year arrived, Americans were still in disbelief that the South could take such steps. "The Constitution, which all the states have adopted, makes no provision for the secession of a state, however much she may feel herself aggrieved. It is her duty to try to redress her grievances in the Union," noted the *News-Letter.* "The present rebellion will probably terminate after much bloodshed, unless the government of the United States consents to let the secessionists have their own way and go out of the Union without opposition." They worried about Lincoln's inauguration—his election was the only reason given by the Southern states for disunion.

"There is nothing of importance transpiring now, except the disunion movement which is the topic of conversation in every circle," wrote Exeter resident B. Judson Perkins in his diary. On March 4, he noted, "This is a beautiful day. Pres. Lincoln was inaugurated today without any opposition. It was celebrated in this town by the ringing of bells and firing cannon."

The new president made no overt moves to eliminate slavery, but the South still threatened to leave the Union. When a brief mention was

TUESDAY, JANUARY 1, 1861.

B. Judson Perkins noted in his diary on January 1, 1861: "There is nothing of importance transpiring now, except the disunion movement which is the topic of conversation in every circle."

made that the Exeter Town Hall had settled slightly into its foundation, the *News-Letter*'s editor used it to make a point: "Perhaps the basement is seceding, who knows? Gravitation admits of no compromises with her principles, and Constitutions should not. The Court would rule, that the walls should be coerced by bolts and bars; indeed this would be a decision of habit."

When the war actually began in April, Exeter was quite clear on why it was happening: the South was in rebellion against the Union because it feared for its system of slavery. It was a Constitutional requirement that the Union be maintained, and that was what drew young men to join the army and the general population to support the effort.

"Our country has cost us too much blood and is of too much value to ourselves and to the world, to be sacrificed to a lawless band of desperadoes," wrote a clergyman from Exeter in an open letter to the president. Elias Nason, pastor at the First Congregational Church in town, preached a fiery war sermon the week after war was declared in which he pronounced, "Down with the Rebellion! The South of this great country is on fire for war. Rebellion anarchy and ruffianism on the one hand; liberty, law and order on the other. Our nation's flag has been insulted; our integrity broken and hatred and full defiance backed with cannon in the hands of traitors, hurled against the supporters of the law."

New Hampshire didn't have a trained army when war broke out, and it took some time to get one organized. In late May, the first group of Exeter men left town. "The volunteers who have enlisted at Exeter N.H. and been residing here for some time, left Saturday afternoon for Portsmouth. They were escorted by the Exeter cornet Band to the railroad station, and followed by the company of Students of the Academy, who have been in the practice of drilling for several weeks past," reported the *News-Letter.*

The war had begun, and Exeter committed itself to preserving the Union. The problem of slavery didn't seem to be the immediate cause of the conflict in 1861. Even Exeter historian Charles Bell titled his chapter on the Civil War "The War for the Union." But patriotism ran high, as one incident in the *News-Letter* attests: "On Thursday morning last, as a butcher from South Newmarket was stopping near the Post Office in this town, one of the soldiers lately enlisted placed a small flag, the Stars and Stripes, in the horse's harness. This so incensed the butcher, that he took down the flag, and rent it in pieces. The last seen of said butcher he was fleeing down Stratham road at 240 speed, with about 30 of the soldiers following him."

HARRIET PATIENCE DAME AND THE SECOND NEW HAMPSHIRE REGIMENT

In 1901, the New Hampshire state legislature, prompted by Governor Frank Rollins, voted to appropriate funds to have a portrait of Civil War nurse Harriet Patience Dame painted and placed in the statehouse. Hers was the first portrait of a woman displayed in such a manner in New Hampshire. Attached to the Second New Hampshire Regiment, she served from the beginning of the war in April 1861 until she mustered out in December 1865—without furlough through two enlistment periods.

Harriet Dame was born in Barnstead, New Hampshire, in 1815. Harriet remained the unmarried daughter, staying with her parents

Civil War nurse Harriet Patience Dame (1815–1900) wasn't from Exeter, but she was beloved by the Second New Hampshire Regiment, which was composed of men from Concord and Exeter.

into her adulthood and moving with them to Concord. She cared for both parents as they aged. After her mother's death in 1854, she purchased a house for herself and her father and took charge of the household until his death in 1859. For a time, she opened her home as a boardinghouse, but with the outbreak of war in 1861, Harriet felt that she had a more important duty.

Like most women, Harriet had never formally trained as a nurse. Her experience running a household and caring for invalids, however, made her an excellent candidate for the nursing corps. At forty-six, she was well within Superintendent of Army Nurses Dorothea Dix's requirement that army nurses be "matronly persons of experience, good conduct, of superior education and serious disposition." Dix also warned, "Only women of strong health, not subjects of chronic disease, nor liable to sudden illnesses, need apply. The duties of the station make large and continued demands on strength." This was no job for fragile or faint women.

Dame's first months of service kept her in Concord ministering to the new recruits. Most New Hampshire men had never strayed far from home. The first weeks in a crowded army camp exposed them to illnesses they'd never encountered before. Measles quickly broke out, along with the near-constant ailments of camp life: diarrhea, dysentery and typhoid fever. After the regiment moved on to Portsmouth for training, Harriet remained in Concord to care for the stragglers.

The Second Regiment was composed mostly of men from Concord and Exeter. Their leader was Colonel Gilman Marston, a fifty-year-old lawyer from Exeter. In late July, the regiment saw action at the First Battle of Bull Run. By that time, Harriet had caught up with "her boys." A fellow member of the regimental medical team, Dr. Joseph Janvrin (like Marston an Exeter man), wrote of the battle to his sister, Abby: "When we were fired upon at Bull Run on our retreat we were the last team and had four wounded men with us. We had to take out our horses and leave the ambulance saving the men and horses only. The cannon ball passed through the body of the carriage just as the horses were being taken out, it went on over the horses' heads." Marston was seriously injured during the engagement. "I had the care of Col. Marston and Captain Rollins from Centreville to Washington," Janvrin wrote. "Both were wounded. Marston's right arm being shattered and Captain Rollins' left shoulder the same. Both will survive and the limbs be saved." Marston would never forget the care provided by Harriet Dame. "She was always present when most needed, and to the suffering, whether Yank or Greyback—it made no difference—she was truly an angel of mercy."

During the ensuing years of the war, Harriet kept up with the regiment, often close to the action. She wrote later, "I have often dodged the shells when on the field. And once at Fair Oaks, Virginia, a shell struck my tent. I happened to be out at the time with Dr. Janvrin making some gruel over the campfire. Dr. Janvrin and I dodged at the same time and we hit our heads together so hard that each of us thought the shell had struck us." She was captured twice by the enemy, each time talking her way out and respectfully being escorted back across lines.

At the war's end, there was still a great deal of work to do. Soldiers were still recovering, and Harriet Dame remained in service until December 1865. When she returned to New Hampshire, a grateful state legislature voted her a $500 bonus—most of which she donated to the Second Regiment to build the headquarters at Weirs Beach. For the remainder of her life, she lived and worked in Washington, D.C., at the Treasury Department, returning to New Hampshire only in 1900, her final year. In 1884, Dorothea Dix founded the Army Nurses Association, and Harriet Dame served as its first president.

That same year, as Congress considered providing pensions to army nurses, Gilman Marston wrote of her, "Miss Dame is the bravest woman I ever knew. I have seen her face a battery without flinching, while a man took refuge behind her to avoid the flying fragments of bursting shells. Of all the men and women who volunteered to serve their country [in] the late war, no one is more deserving of reward than Harriet P. Dame."

GEORGE LEWIS STOKELL: EXETER'S ONE-ARMED POSTMASTER

When Ruth Stokell Challis wrote her essay "I Grew Up in New Hampshire" in 1944, she mentioned her father as a kind man who gave her a set of encyclopedias for her birthday. The large, ever-expanding Stokell family lived on the outskirts of town on Epping Road, near Old Town Farm Road. She recalled that "one of the earliest things I remember is the birth of one of my sisters." It was the kind of memory that would be repeated often, as her mother gave birth to eleven children, eight of whom survived to adulthood.

Ruth's memories about growing up in Exeter in the late 1800s included stories of school and play and losing (and later finding) a little sister. She mentions her parents as a child might, with little specific detail. She left out the most obvious feature of her father: he had only one arm. One might think that a one-armed father would be an

The staff of the Exeter Post Office poses for a photograph in 1905. Sitting in the center is Postmaster George Stokell (1846–1931), a Civil War veteran who had lost his right arm during the Battle of the Wilderness and was later imprisoned at Andersonville.

interesting part of one's childhood, but to Ruth he was simply "Father." The arm, or lack thereof, didn't seem to matter much.

George Lewis Stokell was born in Lowell, Massachusetts, on April 1, 1846. His father, also named George Stokell, headed for California in search of gold in 1849 and told tales of the gold fields for the rest of his life. He didn't strike it rich, however, and returned home to his family, moving them to Portsmouth, New Hampshire, where he worked in the building and construction industry. Young George was quick to sign up when the Civil War broke out. He enlisted in 1861, at age seventeen, in his birth state of Massachusetts with the Eighteenth Massachusetts Regiment and reenlisted three years later.

The war took him to most of the engagements of the Army of the Potomac, including the Second Battle of Bull Run, Chancellorsville and Gettysburg. While fighting in the Battle of the Wilderness in Spotsylvania, Virginia, in May 1864, his regiment lost track of him. He was listed as "missing in action" and was presumed dead. The Wilderness was the first battle that pitted General Ulysses S. Grant against General Robert E. Lee. Both sides saw heavy casualties.

After the battle, the Confederate army found Stokell still alive on the field. His right arm had been shot. Ruth would later write (not in her memoir but in a letter to her daughter) that "the old soldiers did not like to talk about those things, and he had a hell of a time. He had a gold ring like an old wide gold band his mother had given him. The Doctor took it off his right hand and put it on his left finger" shortly before his right arm was amputated. He told his daughter, "If it hadn't been for the Southern Women, coming nights to give him hot soup, and food, dressings and such he would have died."

After his recovery, Stokell became a prisoner of war for nine long months. Imprisoned at various camps, including Andersonville, Lynchburg, Danville, Florence and Charleston, Stokell survived and was repatriated during a prisoner exchange. Conditions in the camps were so harrowing, so appalling, that Stokell couldn't bring himself to talk about it in his later years. All he told his children, according to Ruth, was that "they were starving, Southerners and prisoners."

He was discharged in March 1865, just one month before the war ended. He returned to Boston to take up business but later returned to New Hampshire, where his parents were living. In 1882, already a widower with a young son, he bought a farm on Epping Road in Exeter and married Alberta Carroll, the twenty-year-old daughter of Exeter's Dr. Albert Carroll. Alberta was a graduate of the Robinson Female Seminary. The farm was able to support the growing family for many years. When the Town of Exeter decided to close down the District Three School on Epping Road because of low attendance, Alberta simply set up her own schoolroom and taught the children at home.

For decades after the war, it was common to appoint veterans to public office. In 1904, according to historian Nancy Merrill, "The office of postmaster became a matter of rivalry between the current postmaster, George N. Julian, and Judge Thomas Leavitt. About forty influential citizens sent a petition to President Theodore Roosevelt favoring a third candidate, George L. Stokell, Jr. Stokell's nomination appealed to the president and was accepted by the Senate. Mr. Stokell began his new duties on April 1, 1904."

The family moved to Gill Street to be closer to the public schools and the post office. Stokell served the town as postmaster for eight years, a well-deserved reward for his army service. When his final term was up, he moved to Medford, Massachusetts, where he became commander of the Grand Army of the Republic post. In 1931, at the age of eighty-seven, the old soldier died. He'd been looking forward to marching in one last Memorial Day parade, but he missed it by two weeks. The flags in Medford were put at half-staff in his honor.

PART IV

River Views

Exeter exists because of the rivers. The meeting of the Squamscott and Exeter Rivers at Great Falls is the very center of town and town life. Over the centuries, the rivers have been a source of food, power, transportation and recreation for the people who cling to the banks. Our status as an inland town with a port to the sea has made Exeter unique, and yet there have been times when this very feature has tripped us up and complicated our lives.

Schooners in Exeter

"The three-masted schooner, Benjamin T. Biggs of Exeter, H.W. Anderson controlling owner, was abandoned Sunday in a water logged condition 55 miles south-west of Seguin, an island off the mouth of the Kennebec," related the *Exeter News-Letter* in July 1900. The *Biggs* was a frequent visitor to the wharves of Exeter, hauling coal by the ton for H.W. Anderson. But it didn't survive the trip down the Kennebec River. When Anderson traveled to Maine to check on his schooner, it was too late.

The Squamscott River connects to Great Bay and ultimately the Atlantic Ocean. In the early part of the nineteenth century, salt, bricks, paper, fish, cotton and textiles made their way up and down the

A schooner being towed on the Squamscott River.

Squamscott in elegant schooners. The final miles were accomplished with the help of a tugboat, as the twisting nature of the riverbed made navigation difficult. On the river, the schooners faced few risks. Out at sea, the trip could be far more perilous.

The *Mary Manning* hauled coal for H.W. Anderson, but this wasn't the only type of cargo it hauled. In 1900, it was carrying a full load of ice out of Bangor, Maine, when it grounded at the mouth of the Penobscot River. The inquest placed the blame firmly on the tugboat *Seguin*, which had allowed too much towing line. The ship wasn't badly damaged and was soon put to work again. In March 1906, the *Mary Manning* left Florida with a full load of yellow pine and railroad ties, headed for New York. Off the coast of Boston, a gale blew up, and the ship was struck by lightning. "Before the storm had reached its height a bolt struck the main boom, which broke off, carrying away the mainsail and foretopmast staysail. The vessel was swamped by heavy seas and all the boats were swept away or smashed. The schooner carried a donkey engine to hoist the sails, but a giant sea flooded the engine room, smashed the forward house, and ruined all the provisions except the canned goods," reported the *New York Times* on March 7.

The ship soon sprung a leak, and the desperate crew tried to keep it afloat for 110 hours. "With two of his ribs beaten in by a shifting deckload of lumber, Ingebard Gjerteen, a Norwegian sailor, dived from the wrecked *Mary Manning*, a four-masted schooner, in the height of a gale on Saturday last, and saved the life of Joseph Arie of Waretown, N.J., the mate, who had become delirious and jumped overboard," the *Times* continued. The ship was going down when the crew was rescued by the *Casilda*. All hands were saved, but their condition was "so grave that it was difficult to keep life in them." The *Mary Manning* was last seen sinking to the bottom of the sea.

Anderson's *Benjamin T. Biggs* didn't fare much better. Loaded with Maine lumber for New York, it, like the *Manning*, hit a gale and was quickly swamped. The crew was picked up seventeen hours later. The *Exeter News-Letter* quoted Captain Tibbetts as saying, "When we left the vessel she was beginning to break up forward and at one place in the cabin floor. We had quite a rough experience. We saved only our dunnage." Tugs were sent out to tow the ship to shore, but Anderson found that his ship—which should have been able to be recovered—was destroyed by the rescuers.

By the time the wreck was towed back to Rockland, "attempt had previously been made to burn her as a dangerous derelict, and she was ablaze when picked up. As a result of this fire, which destroyed her deck and upper works, the *Biggs* is a hopeless wreck, and only her anchors and chains can be saved," reported the *News-Letter*. Anderson had lost one of his most dependable schooners. The following year, he began hiring sturdy gundalows to haul coal. "Each year sees a diminution in the number of small schooners and Mr. Anderson finds it difficult to charter all he needs. He has been compelled to have 600 tons of coal delivered at Portsmouth to be brought up river by his own and chartered gundalows," the *News-Letter* noted.

Within two decades, most of the coal used in Exeter would be brought in by rail and freight trucks. They may not have had the majesty of the schooners, but they were much safer for the crews.

THE SQUAMSCOTT OXBOW

When John Wheelwright first arrived in Exeter in March 1638, he complained of the deep snows that he had to traverse: "[I]t was marvelous that I got thither at that time…by reason of the deep snow in which I might have perished." He waited a few months before sending for his wife and children so that they could make the trip more easily by boat. As she traveled up the Squamscott, Mary Hutchinson Wheelwright must have wondered about the unusual course the river took as it made its way to the headwaters at the falls, where her husband was waiting.

About three miles out of town, the river took an unexpected twist to the right and, just as suddenly, looped back to the original path. This loop would trouble navigators for the next 250 years.

Called an oxbow, the loop is a natural formation caused by meandering of the riverbed. Sometimes an oxbow can curl all the way around, stranding the land in the center. The Squamscott oxbow showed no signs of closing at the base. Its only contribution to Exeter's busy seaport was to snarl up river traffic.

Exeter residents traveled the river in small craft until the 1700s, when shipbuilding became an important industry in town. The river was deep enough to accommodate ships, provided they could be transported downstream to Great Bay. That oxbow—or "great roundabout," as it was sometimes called—created no end of trouble. To navigate the double twists in a time before motorized engines, the crew would resort to pushing the vessel with long poles or casting the anchor forward and pulling it to get around the bends. William Saltonstall noted in his *Ports of Piscataqua* that "no wind could have been fickle enough to get a boat equipped with sails through the Great Roundabout," and Olive Tardiff followed this in *Exeter Squamscott: River of Many Uses* with, "Sometimes it was necessary for a vessel to wait as long as a week for favorable winds and tides in order to reach Exeter."

By 1880, Charles Bell observed, "The navigation of the channel had become so obstructed by rocks and shoals that it was found necessary to petition Congress for an appropriation for its improvement." The petition was granted, and it was decided that instead of simply cleaning up the oxbow, it would be cut through. At the point where the looped ends nearly came together, a channel would be dug to allow a straight entrance to Exeter's harbor.

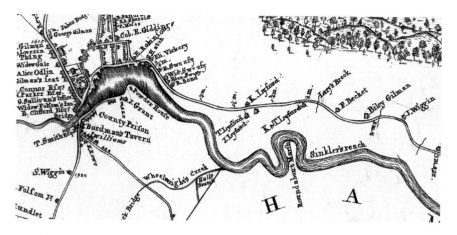

An 1802 map of Exeter by Phineas Merrill shows the troublesome oxbow, here called the "Roundabout Marsh."

Work began in the early fall of 1881. Although it was nothing like the digging of the Panama Canal, it was made more difficult by an unusually hot Indian summer. The *Exeter News-Letter* noted that Wednesday, September 28 was the "hottest day since July 14th." It was muggy and already seventy degrees at sunrise. To get the miserable job done quickly, the *News-Letter* advertised, "It is intended to push the work of cutting off the ox-bow as rapidly as possible, and for that purpose, we are informed, employment will be given to any number of laborers from this town at $1.50 a day. As many hands as are wanted can readily be secured from other places, but the contractor prefers as far as possible to secure his laborers from this town."

You'd think there would have been an excited and jubilant outcry in the newspapers once the oxbow was finally bypassed, but instead the news was silent. It must have been one of those satisfying but nearly invisible triumphs—like cleaning the oven—that affects only a few and excites even fewer. Nonetheless, river traffic picked up for a time, and coal schooners routinely made the trek upriver.

The oxbow was still navigable by small boats after the cut was made. John Hurlbert wrote an account of a schooner trip up the Squamscott in 1897, noting, "A short way down from Exeter there is a triple bend of the river which is called the oxbow. The river winds from shore to shore in graceful curves, but grace and utility cannot always be combined, so a few years ago there was a channel cut close to the right bank. As we sailed down between the high banks of clay we envied the little boat that flitted around the curves, dipping in the breeze like a swallow, and doubtless the occupants envied us as they put about to look at us."

Fun, perhaps, for a small pleasure craft at the time, but today the oxbow is nearly gone. It can be viewed from above or by zooming in on Google Earth. From the river, if one is in a kayak or canoe, the entrances to the oxbow are tantalizingly broad enough to lure the paddler in. But unless you are very adept at back-paddling, it is inadvisable to attempt to navigate the entire oxbow. After several hundred feet of pretty surroundings and tall grass, the channel narrows until the kayak becomes mired in the spongy undergrowth and shallow water. The wildlife of the area will offer no assistance to the desperate paddler and will only mock you with deep-throated croaking. I did get out, eventually, a tired but wiser adventurer.

THE PERILOUS VOYAGE OF THE *LIZZIE J. CALL*

By the dawn of the twentieth century, river shipping on the Squamscott had declined to a trickle. In earlier times, the river was necessary to haul raw materials to town for the factories and mills. The Exeter Manufacturing Company shipped raw cotton upriver and then sent finished cloth out to market. The Flagg and Wiswall paper mill brought in loads of rags to make into paper, and the town's many merchants used the river to bring in goods from Boston.

But by the mid-1800s, the railroad had taken over most of the transportation of goods. Newer factories were built on the western part of town, clustered around the depot. The only materials shipped on the Squamscott were heavy goods—lumber, coal and bricks—that were still best moved by water.

Harry Anderson didn't give up on the river. By the turn of the century, the town had developed an insatiable hunger for coal. Coal ran the steam machinery of the Exeter Manufacturing Company. It heated the homes, schools and public buildings in town. Exeter's Eagle Steamer fire engine pumped seven thousand gallons of water per minute through the use of a coal-fired engine. Anderson was well aware that the cheapest and quickest way to transport hundreds of tons

The schooner *Lizzie J. Call.*

of coal was by water. In 1893, he almost single-handedly revived river transport for a brief period of time.

Anderson had a great love of sailing and put this to good use by bringing his coal supplies upriver on schooners. Nancy Merrill, in her *Exeter, New Hampshire: 1888–1988*, states that he "at one time owned five schooners home-berthed in Exeter"; one of these was the *Lizzie J. Call.*

Built in Portsmouth in 1886, the *Lizzie J. Call* had a regular crew of five, including the captain. During the six-month-long coal strike of 1902, it brought in the last load of anthracite coal—preferred for heating because it burned hotter and smoked less than soft coal. But even that load wasn't quite enough. "Schooner *Lizzie J. Call* arrived Saturday morning with 250 tons of broken coal for H.W. Anderson, her managing owner. It was bought the day before the coal strike, 300 tons not being available," reported the *Exeter News-Letter.* During the next six months, only inferior soft coal was available, and this was snatched up by the Exeter Manufacturing Company and the town. Anderson scrambled to purchase coal from Wales, but only at an increased price. When the Pennsylvanian coal miners finally resolved the strike in mid-October, it took another month before coal became available to householders.

The *Lizzie J. Call* nearly met its end in 1908. The *Exeter News-Letter* reported on June 5, "After narrowly escaping being sent to the bottom by passing steamers on three different occasions, the three-masted schooner, *Lizzie J. Call*, of Exeter, was driven ashore on the rocks at Winthrop, Massachusetts, during the gale early Sunday morning, and those on board gave up all hope of rescue." Heading out of Perth Amboy, New Jersey, with a load of 278 tons of coal, the ship had encountered dense fog—so dense that three times they were almost struck by passing ships. The gale increased, and the ship soon found itself in great danger. The *Exeter News-Letter* account tells what happened next:

> *They were peering through the mist when suddenly the vessel crashed onto the rocks off Winthrop at 12:30 Sunday morning and her masts nearly went by the board when she struck. She was thrown higher up on the beach by the tremendous seas, and the waves beat against her hull and dashed high into the rigging. The men on board were drenched to the skin, and they clung to the rigging to prevent being swept into the sea.*
>
> *The vessel pounded so badly that her seams opened and she began to leak. The tug Leader happened along and seeing the predicament of the vessel ran down to render assistance. A heavy hawser was made fast to the vessel and the tug straightened out and pulled on her. After considerable tugging the schooner began to move and she was soon hauled into deep water.*

The ship had taken on so much water that even after its rescue from the rocks, it was still in danger. The bilge pumps barely kept it afloat long enough to make it to port in East Boston. There it was repaired enough to make it home to Exeter.

The *Lizzie J. Call* continued to travel up and down the Squamscott River until barges and trucks proved to be more efficient. Anderson sold his coal company to William McReel in 1910. McReel preferred to ship his coal from Portsmouth and Kittery by barge, and the swift-running schooners were no longer needed for long trips at sea. Once coal faded from use in the late 1940s, the days of dusty coal mounds piled alongside the river were over. The days of the schooners on the Squamscott River were also over.

THE GRAND REGATTA

In 1872, there were more than 150 regattas held in North America. The schoolboys of Phillips Exeter Academy decided that they should hold a regatta of their own. The Boat Club at the academy was still in its infancy and had not yet begun to encourage rowing as a team sport.

Exeter's downtown merchants still shipped goods up and down the river in 1872. Gundalows carried lumber, bricks and fish, and schooners were towed into the harbor with tons of coal. Alongside the commercial traffic were many different types of small boats. Some were pleasure boats; others were tough little rowboats and canoes used by sportsmen for fishing and hunting. True rowing sculls, as we are used to seeing today, were rare on the river.

They set their "Grand Regatta" for a Wednesday afternoon in late spring. Then, as now, students at the academy had only a half day of classes on Wednesdays and Saturdays. The afternoon was free, and the boys were only lightly supervised. They scrounged boats from wherever they could and determined to hold four separate races.

The first race was single scull. Four boys were set to start the race, but when the starting lineup was called, two of them dropped out. "Harwood and Hodges, nursing their strength to keep it fresh for the four-oared race, failed to make their appearance," reported the *Exeter News-Letter.* Perhaps they were unable to find a boat small enough for the race. The remaining two racers, Charles Bell (class of 1872) and Robert Blodgett (class of 1873), had decidedly different types of boats. Blodgett had a racing scull, but the best Bell was able to come up with was a heavy dory called a "wherry." He'd fitted it out with racing outriggers to hold the oars high above the water, but it still wasn't up to the challenge. The judges generously gave him a twelve-second handicap.

The *News-Letter's* fledgling attempt at sports writing read as follows: "The word 'go' is sounded, and the race begins. Blodgett with a firm and steady stroke pulls as for dear life; Bell keeps along space, when a sad mishap occurs; his out-riggers break, and Blodget wins the race and the prize, a silver ladle; time, 6.58; course, 1¼ miles."

Three boys were entered in the sailboat race, but as in the first race, not all of them made it to the starting line. William Swift of New Bedford, Massachusetts, didn't quite get there in time with his lapstreak centerboard boat. Lapstreak (or "lapstrake") boats are made with

The Phillips Exeter Academy 1921 crew team. *Courtesy of Phillips Exeter Academy.*

Phillips Exeter Academy crew team, 1866. *Courtesy of Phillips Exeter Academy.*

overlapping planking, like a Viking boat. They're strong but slightly less agile in the water. The two remaining boats in the sailing race were a flat-bottomed boat called *Mary Jane*, captained by Trueman Heminway (class of 1873), and the keel-bottomed *Flying Dutchman*, with Isaiah Thomas (class of 1872) at the helm.

The *Flying Dutchman* took an early lead but ran aground on the third tack, leaving the *Mary Jane* as the only survivor to cross the finish line. Heminway won a silvered fruit dish as his prize.

Neither of these first two races satisfied the onlookers—considering both had been won due to mechanical problems. The real race of the day was the four-oared contest. Two teams readied themselves for the race: the *Una*, a lapstreak racing shell representing the class of 1872, and the *Wyoma*, entered by the class of 1873. Both carried crews of five boys—four rowers and one coxswain. "While the *Una* crew boasts the best oar—Jones, the popular man of his class, the *Wyoma*'s friends rely upon the unyielding pluck of her crew; and even feign to believe that intelligence and scholarship must count in their favor," observed the *News-Letter*. But intelligence would not rule the day. The *Una* quickly outpaced the *Wyoma* to win the race a full minute ahead. Each boy was awarded a prize cup.

The final race of the Grand Regatta was a tub race:

> *The gazing throng now prepare for a laughing excitement; for the tub race is announced. Six ordinary tubs are launched upon the water, and the sportive youths enter the same, each "to paddle his own canoe" to gain the coveted prizes. The leaky and unstable condition of the novel vessels results in many an overturn and apparently sinking hopes; but a cooled person and uncooled ardor lead to braver exertions, and the race is won by Brown of '74; Harwood of '73 was ahead most of the time, but a luckless foul with another boat, when nearing the shore, lost to him the prize.*

The winner received two dollars—perhaps by this time they were fresh out of silver kitchenware to award.

For all its mishaps, the Grand Regatta was pronounced a success, and for years afterward, at least until rowing became a more organized sport at Phillips Exeter Academy, a regatta was held each spring.

PART V

The Supernatural

Were there any mysterious occurrences in Exeter? For such an old town, we have remarkably few haunted stories to tell. Perhaps this is because the curator of the Exeter Historical Society sees little value in ghost stories, based as they are on unprovable beliefs and vague creepy feelings. Get a hold of yourself and accept that old houses are noisy and drafty! However, if you prefer, here are a few slightly unearthly stories to relate around the campfire.

A Fine Undertaking

When Exeter's large cemetery on Linden Street was created in 1843, it was designed to be park-like—a place one might stroll through on a warm afternoon. It was a far cry from the stark graveyards of earlier times. Funeral rites and furnishings had changed considerably since the town's settlement in 1638, and the new cemetery reflected some of those changes.

When John Wheelwright and his small band of Puritan dissenters first arrived in Exeter, the necessary graveyard was located near the meetinghouse, somewhere in the vicinity of Salem Street. The grave markers of these earliest residents are gone now. Most likely, they

Field Furniture shop on Main Street in Exeter. It was not uncommon to see "furniture and undertaking" advertised at the same establishment.

weren't marked well, and when the new meetinghouse was built in the center of town, the graveyard was abandoned.

Not that it would have been a pleasant place to visit. Puritans considered one's mortal remains to be relatively unimportant. Death brought with it a frightening uncertainty about a loved one's eternal soul. No one knew whom God had elected to salvation or damnation, and this terror of the grave was reflected on the carvings that can still be viewed on older headstones. A quick walk through the Winter Street cemetery will reveal numerous examples of the "winged death's head"—a cold reminder of man's mortality—on the stones. The people buried are never "beloved" or "dear"; in fact, the men are never described at all, they're just a name with dates attached. Women are nearly always attached in some way to a man. She's a "widow of," "wife of," "consort of" or even "relict of" someone else. Rarely is she her own person, even in death.

Children—and there are a startling number of children buried in the Winter Street cemetery—are treated the same way as adults, with the same type of headstone art. Children weren't sheltered from death; it was all around them. When one of their playmates died, the children were part of the funeral rite and frequently carried the coffin of their friend to the graveyard. This was done to remind them of their own mortality. They didn't fool around back then.

Over time, the harshness of the Puritan worldview began to melt. The flying skull softened into a winged cherub, and later an urn and willow took the place at the top of headstones. By the time the Exeter Cemetery was laid out, there were no more harsh symbols to be found. Funeral practices and care of the dead began to change as well.

When John W. Field opened his undertaking business in Exeter in 1895, it had evolved into a specialized field. In previous decades, the dead were simply washed and laid in a crude homemade coffin in preparation for burial. In the United States, the Civil War changed this practice.

During prior wars, fallen soldiers were simply buried where they'd fallen. It was a rare, and usually wealthy, family who were able to retrieve their dead. Admiral Horatio Lord Nelson, who was killed at the Battle of Trafalgar, was famously preserved in a cask of rum until his fleet returned to London. But his treatment was rare. More often, soldiers' remains were returned years later after temporary interment. By then, there was little left but dried bones.

During the Civil War, the railroad allowed quick transportation for the fallen. It was quick but not quick enough to fend off the obvious effects of decomposition. Ice proved to be impractical for a trip of several weeks, so surgeons began to use various concoctions to preserve the body long enough for the trip and subsequent funeral. Formaldehyde wasn't discovered until after the war, so these early embalmers tried other substances such as arsenic, creosote, mercury, turpentine or alcohol. It's no wonder that the embalming profession itself had a high mortality rate. As crude as the practices were, grieving families were grateful to have their loved ones returned home, and embalming became nearly standard practice in North America.

With this greater care of dead came a desire for more elegant coffins. The traditional shape, six sides tapered at the shoulders, gave way to a rectangular casket that looked more like a piece of fine furniture. The field specialized as a branch of cabinetmaking, which was why John Field's business was Fine Furniture and Undertaking. Today, we'd never think of going to a furniture store to pick up a casket, but it didn't seem morbid at all in 1900.

Casket selection, interior of Field Furniture shop in Exeter.

Although some funerals were still held in private homes in the early 1900s, the advent of the funeral parlor made the practice less common. Caskets ceased to be sold in furniture stores, so you could no longer browse through stacks of them while shopping for a new dining room set. Field's undertaking services ceased to be listed in Exeter's business directory by 1920, and by the 1940s, there are almost no home funerals listed in obituaries. Death had become quite separate from the everyday world of the living.

THE CURIOUS CASE OF THE
PARK STREET HAUNTINGS

Old houses are very noisy places to live. Floors creak. Bedroom doors open or shut spontaneously on uneven hinges. Changes in humidity can create odd popping sounds. During daylight hours, the racket is hardly noticeable. But when night falls and everyone is settled in, the house becomes the enemy. Is it any wonder that the Exeter Historical Society gets frequent calls from people who want to track down the house ghost?

If you really, truly want a house ghost, we can probably find one for you. If the house is old, someone probably died there; with a little research, we can track down the type of ghost you'd like: widower, spinster, child or old gray mare.

Considering the age of the town, it's a wonder we don't have more documented haunted houses, but the archives at the Exeter Historical Society reveal only one case. In a lengthy, rambling document, Isaac Bradford recorded "An Account of Physical Manifestations at House in Exeter, N.H. July 1879." His actual address does not appear anywhere in print during the time he lived in town, which is very frustrating when one is trying to track down the exact location of a potentially haunted house, but it was probably somewhere near Park Street.

Bradford was a mathematician who traveled to Boston frequently. In the summer of 1879, he was living in Exeter with his wife, Jane; daughter, Nellie; and young son, Isaac Jr. (called "Ikey" in the account). Also in the house were Annie, Eva and Ben. Ben seems to have been a young man—he is always given his own room; Annie was an adult and Eva a child. Mary, a maid, slept in the attic.

On July 14, Bradford returned from a trip to Boston. The weather was hot, and the family fitfully went to bed. The previous night, they informed him, they'd heard raps and loud noises all night. Bradford sat up in his study to get some work done, and just as they'd described it, loud rappings were heard in the upstairs bedchambers. The noisiest room was occupied by Jane and Annie. The noise seemed to stop whenever Bradford entered, so the ladies moved to another room, and he remained behind, dozing in a chair:

> *I went into my wife's room and put my ear to the wall from whence the noise proceeded, sitting in a chair against it. As I said the noise ceased, but I heard a curious ringing, singing, crackling sound inside of the wall as I thus sat. Then I kind of half dozed, and saw a woman dressed in white peasant cut short dress, with large sunflap bonnet on seem to be going away and as she went she turned round and waved her hand "goodbye."*

The next night, the rapping returned, but Bradford had traced the trouble to the casters on the bed. He removed them from the "troublesome bedstead," and there was peace in the house for several weeks. He must not have had any ghostly half-dreams either because he didn't mention any.

On August 1, the weather was again hot and the noises returned. This time, the family members played musical rooms—each trying to move away from the noises. The little girls moved up to the attic to escape, only to waken Mary, the maid, who then began to hear raps as well. Had she not been awakened by the girls, she probably would have slept through the entire incident. Instead, she was so frightened that she couldn't get back to sleep and began to see things moving about in the room.

Another very hot day followed. Bradford went to bed at about 2:00 a.m., only to be awakened soon after by Annie, Ikey and Nellie. Ikey had heard someone banging on the door outside, and the others were frightened. Bradford went outside but could find no one. The noises continued all that night and the following night:

> *My wife on the bedstead, and Annie on the floor, heard the most curious noises. Annie inquired what they were. My wife suggested that they proceeded from the casters which were lying upon the floor, one at each corner of the bed. The lamp was lit, and a caster placed by Annie under the center of the bedstead. The moment the light was put out the caster flew across the room striking the wall.*

Bradford, man of science that he was, pondered the cause of the disruptions. "I had thought at first that it was the resounding of the horse's kicking in the barn attached to the house, but more probably it is due to the electricity developed through the heat of the house." However, he seemed uncertain about this theory, ending his piece, "Monday morning when Annie came to depart the house banged with such violence as to be heard by the Cilley's opposite. Annie went across to Mrs. C's and the noises ceased. Miss Cilley was in our house and she and my wife heard the noises resumed, and discovered that Annie had returned and gone upstairs unknown to them. When she arrived home, she went and passed the night with a friend, and that house banged also."

Bradford ends his account with the departure of Annie. Perhaps she was the one who brought the troublesome noises, or maybe it was the heat or the bewitched bed casters. We'll never know for sure, and no further accounts of the hauntings from Park Street have been reported. Troublesome noises heard at night are best resolved by acquiring a cat. Not only will the cat keep any mice from the walls, but any unusual nocturnal sound can be blamed on its movements. And cats are never bothered by ghosts.

RAINESFORD ROGERS AND THE WHITE CAPS

Tucked away in the back of Charles Bell's *History of the Town of Exeter, New Hampshire* is a small anecdote about a group of treasure hunters who were duped by a transient rogue named Rainesford Rogers. Bell was a cautious historian who wouldn't have included the story if he wasn't sure it was true, but he also didn't want to embarrass the people involved. And so we have a somewhat funny story that, due to Bell's reticence, has few verifiable elements.

In the tale, Rogers arrives in town and is able to convince about a dozen Exeter men that there is treasure buried somewhere within the town limits. The men formed a work gang, and night after night they followed Rogers into the woods and swamps to dig for gold. That they never found anything didn't seem to have discouraged any of them, nor did it make them question Rogers's ability to pick the sites for digging.

In 1800, around the time this incident seems to have occurred, Exeter was still a strict Protestant town. Parish taxes were collected, and church membership was considered a civic duty. But within this stringent society there was still an undercurrent of the occult. "White magic" practitioners were occasional visitors to the landscape and were granted a certain amount of credibility. These people, sometimes known as "cunning folk," were contacted to help find lost items or to locate water by dowsing. Among the many types of cunning folk were money-diggers. Tracing their trade back to ancient alchemistic traditions, it was commonly believed that mists and gasses deep within the earth produced hordes of precious metals, particularly mercury and gold. Or the belief might have been that there were piles of gold coins buried by the ancients or even pirates. However it may have gotten there wasn't as important as the absolute fact that there was gold in them thar hills.

Dark, woody places such as this in Exeter were even darker a few hundred years ago, before public lighting. The disorientation this led to and the superstitions of the population made it easier for Rainesford Rogers to dupe his marks.

The Money Diggers, by John Quidor. *Used by permission of the Brooklyn Museum.*

The *New Hampshire Sentinel* reported in 1822:

> *Every country has its money diggers, who are full in the belief that vast treasures lay concealed in the earth. So far from being a new project, it dates its origin with the first man who ever wielded a spade. Even in these latter days, we find men so much in love with the "root of all evil" and so firm in the belief that it may be dug up, that they will traverse hill and dale, climb the loftiest mountain, and even work their way into the bowels of the earth in search of it. Indeed digging for money hid in the earth, is a very common thing; and in this State, it is even considered an honorable and profitable employment.*

So perhaps it's not too surprising that Rogers was able to convince the treasure hunters in Exeter that quick riches only required some digging.

What the Exeter men didn't know was that Rainesford Rogers had a long history of swindling gullible people out of their own money. He'd been involved in a well-publicized scheme in New Jersey that was published in a book called *The Morris-Town Ghost: An Account of the Beginning, Transactions and Discovery of Ransford Rogers, Who Seduced Many by Pretended Hobgoblins and Apparitions, and Thereby Extorted Money from Their Pockets* in 1788. He slipped away from Morris County, changed his name to "Rice Williams" for a while and continued to ply his trade as a dowser of gold until he arrived in Exeter sometime around 1800. Charles Bell picks up the story from there: "He came to Exeter, bearing his true name of Rainsford Rogers, which had, perhaps, not acquired so bad an odor in New England as in some other quarters." He asked the men to wear white caps while digging, perhaps to make it easier to spot them all in the dark.

At one point in the Exeter escapade, Rogers used a tactic he'd used before: he dressed up as a ghost to further convince the diggers that they were in the right place. The ghost muttered something unintelligible, to which one of the men inquired, "A little louder, Mr. Ghost; I'm rather hard of hearing!" The men dug with renewed enthusiasm.

Bell continued: "After a time Rogers disclosed what he declared to be the reason of their want of success. The golden deposit was there, beyond question; but they needed one thing more to enable them to find and grasp it. That was a particular kind of divining-rod." Naturally, this would cost money. The men raised several hundred dollars and loaned Rogers a horse, and off he rode to Philadelphia (or so they thought), never to be heard from again.

Exeter, being a small town, had long been aware of the midnight digging sessions of the "secret" little group. When it was revealed that Rogers was gone, the men involved received no end of ribbing from the population and were thereafter branded with the moniker "white caps." According to Bell, "The deaf man who required the ghost to 'speak a little louder' never heard the last of his unfortunate speech."

EXETER'S SECRET TUNNELS

Are there secret tunnels in Exeter? Lots of towns have stories about "secret tunnel" systems that a few people say they've seen at some time in the past. Yet none of these mysterious tunnels has ever been found. Most of the stories have connections to the colonial period or the Underground Railroad. Exeter is no exception to this type of legend, and there are two tunnel stories that persist to this day.

Stories about a tunnel in the basement of the Gilman Garrison House begin to surface in about 1900. The house, which sits on the corner of Water and Clifford Streets, was built in 1709 by John Gilman. It changed hands over the years, and by the time the tunnel story appears, it was owned by Jenny Harvey, a local schoolteacher. She and her sister, Asenath Darling, had begun the tradition of showing the house to interested visitors and schoolchildren. In his book about the house, *The Old Logg House by the Bridge*, Robbins Paxton Gilman tackles the legend and mentions that it was, perhaps, egged on by our local schools:

> *Some of our local senior Exeter citizens tell us that they have heard all their lives about the Garrison House tunnel and they assume that a tunnel either exists or has caved in. A few recount how Miss Elizabeth Baker's eight grade class at Exeter's Robinson Female Seminary was taught as a factual matter in the study of New Hampshire history that a tunnel existed in the Garrison House. One lady recalls how she was taken by Miss Baker in the spring on a trip to the house and how the class walked through the tunnel to the river ("It was lined with wood and damp")... "there was a niche in the wall where we were told the colonists stored gunpowder," etc.). Others note how, as children, they used to play in the entrance to the tunnel at the river's edge until older and wiser people closed it up to prevent accidents.*

Exeter's Garrison House, built by the Gilman family in 1709, has long been rumored to have tunnels leading into the basement.

The house was purchased by the Dudley family in 1912, and William Perry Dudley was taken enough with the tunnel story to relate it to children while making classroom visits. In a note in the Exeter Historical Society files, however, his mother, Frances Perry Dudley, remarked, "There is a story that an underground passage led from the house to the river; but there is no trace of it now."

In the 1930s, the United States Department of the Interior undertook a project to document the nation's historic homes. The Garrison home was included in the survey, and great pains were taken to document the architecture and construction. On one map, there is a note explaining the excavations that were made to search for evidence of a tunnel. This same map has dotted lines showing "the location of the tunnel as remembered by various inhabitants." There are three different "tunnels," each leading in a different direction. The study was unable to locate any tunnels. Gilman concluded, as we should also, that "this extraordinary claim may reduce fascinating folklore to absurdity."

There is also no evidence that the Underground Railroad existed anywhere near Exeter. Many of us were nursed through our nation's troubling slave history with calming stories of devoted white Northerners

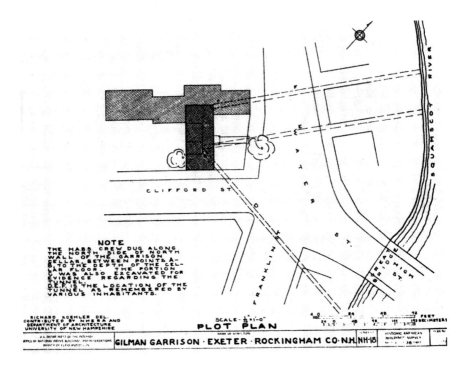

U.S. Department of the Interior map made in the 1930s indicated three different locations townspeople gave for the Garrison House tunnels. No tunnels were ever located.

who hid whole slave families in hidden rooms of houses, spiriting them off to Canada through tunnels with secret signals. There are no accounts in the newspapers or town records from the early nineteenth century to indicate that fugitive slaves were seen or pursued in Exeter. But for many years, children in town were taught that the Odiorne Bickford House on Cass Street was a "station" on the Underground Railroad and that the evidence was a hidden room.

To be fair, there is a hidden room in the house. I've been in it, but it's not so much a hidden room as an architectural feature caused by a dead space around the chimney. Lots of old houses have such spaces. The house seems to have become part of the Underground Railway lore sometime around the 1950s, when the civil rights movement was heating up. During that time, everyone wanted to be part of the Underground Railway, and since there was little documentation about it, every crevasse or attic crawl space was considered proof. The house on Cass Street has a slightly troubled history with slavery in that slaves actually lived there for several decades. Perhaps the story evolved as a means to atone for its earlier history. At some point, the hidden room stuffed full with slaves grew into a passage through the floorboards that led to the basement and a tunnel that led to the river. Let's be clear: there is no tunnel in this house. It sits on sandy soil, and like all the neighboring houses, it has to have a sump pump running nearly all year. There is an underground stream that runs through the yard. The amount of effort it would take to dig and maintain a tunnel would have been extraordinary, not to mention unnecessary considering the house sits roughly one-sixteenth of a mile away from the river.

Why do these stories exist? Are we that gullible, or do we simply like the romance of a tall tale? Peter Smith, who taught at the Exeter Junior High for decades, remembers the tunnel stories well. He summed them up well as "a good gimmick to get kids interested in history, it's gloomy and dark, but probably not too feasible." Perhaps someone will really find a secret tunnel system in Exeter (aside from the very real ones that exist at Phillips Exeter Academy, but that's a story for another time), and we can then marvel at our ancestors' cleverness. But for now, the evidence just isn't there.

PART VI

We the People

J ohn Wheelwright's time in Exeter was short. Many other people have come to Exeter—some stayed and others did not—and all are part of our story. At one time, it was common to hear a cacophony of languages spoken in the factories near the railroad tracks. Sadly, it was also common to hear tales from families who were suffering because of discrimination.

JUDE HALL AND HIS FAMILY

Just off Drinkwater Road, on land owned by Phillips Exeter Academy, there's a small body of water called Jude's Pond. This picturesque site was once the land and home of Jude Hall, a former slave and Revolutionary War veteran. His life story reflects the difficulties that most New England African Americans had to bear in the early republic.

Hall was born in 1747, most likely in Newmarket, and was enslaved first to Philemon Blake and later to Nathaniel Healy. When the Revolution broke out, Hall ran away and joined the Continental army. George Quintal's *Patriots of Color*, which studied the Battles of Bunker Hill and Battle Road, remarked, "This study confirms what the Revolutionary soldiers knew first-hand: the great mass of the 1775 army, excluding officers, was completely integrated. This level of integration did not occur in the Civil War, or for that matter World War II, but only reached similar levels in the Vietnam Conflict nearly two hundred years later." Jude Hall remained with the Continental army for seven years and participated in fighting at Bunker Hill, Ticonderoga, Trenton, Hubbardton, Saratoga and Monmouth. Injured several times, he reenlisted and was discharged in 1783.

Granted his freedom and some land, he settled in Exeter. Exeter's free black population swelled after the war, eventually composing nearly 5 percent of the populace in town. Jude Hall married Rhoda Paul in 1785, and together they had twelve children. Locating records for the family is difficult. Births were not always registered, so it can be difficult to document what happed to their children. Rhoda was descended from a noted Exeter family beginning with her grandfather, Caesar Paul. Caesar had been enslaved in his youth to Major John Gilman and accompanied his master during the French and Indian War. Upon returning to town, he was freed in 1771 and, shortly thereafter, married Lovey Rollins, the daughter of Stratham lawyer Caleb Rollins. Rhoda was one of Caesar and Lovey's ten children. Three of her brothers became noted Baptist preachers.

We know little about the everyday life of Jude and Rhoda. He is described as a "yeoman," or landowning farmer, but it is doubtful that he was ever wealthy. When asked to describe his property to reapply for his military pension in 1820, he listed only "[o]ne small one story house two rooms in it, a few plates, earthen shovel & tongs, a few other articles of furniture of small value."

Hall served as a witness in the murder trial of John Blaisdell in 1822. The murderer, Blaisdell, had brought the victim, John Wadleigh, to Hall's house. Jude assisted the injured man back to his own place and stayed with him through the night until he died. The trial transcript allows us to hear Hall's voice: "After Wadleigh got over his chill and shuddering he said Captain (meaning me) how long have you been here—and then he gave a sithe and was gone again."

Although Jude Hall was trusted enough to testify in court, it was still not possible for free people of color to live unthreatened. Robert Roberts, who had married Jude and Rhoda's eldest daughter, Dorothy, would later testify about the fates of three of the Hall children. James was kidnapped at the age of eighteen from the Hall home. David Wedgewood, of Exeter, claimed that James owed him four dollars and that he was justified in dragging him away from his mother. He was sold into slavery and never returned to Exeter. Roberts said, in 1833, "He was seen, not long since, at New Orleans, by George Ashton, a colored man, from Exeter; he said he was chained up in the calaboose or jail, at New Orleans, as a runaway; and, in the meantime, his master came, and commanded him to be punished severely, and carried him back."

Aaron, another son, put to sea in Providence and signed a promissory note for $20 to pay for his sea clothes. Upon his return, the merchant demanded $200. Roberts related his fate: "He started from Providence to carry his money to his father, and was overtaken to Roxbury, on his way home, and carried back, sent to sea, and has not been heard of since."

William also thought that a seafaring life would offer independence and income and sailed out of Newburyport. "After arriving at the West Indies, was sold there as a slave; and, after remaining in slavery ten years, by some means run away, and is now in England, a captain of a collier from Newcastle to London. About three years ago, his mother heard of him, the first time for upwards of twenty years."

Jude Hall didn't live long enough to hear from William. He died in 1827 at the age of eighty. Rhoda moved to Belfast, Maine, to be with their daughter. She applied for and received the widow's pension for her husband's loyal service in the Revolutionary War. Jude Hall had fought to free a nation but was ultimately unable to see his own children granted freedom.

THE CHINESE EDUCATIONAL MISSION

The rolls of Phillips Exeter Academy students for the 1880s include the names of seven students from China. Their presence here was a unique experiment of the Qing government called the Chinese Educational Mission; it turned out to be both a great success and a great failure.

The original idea behind the mission was to send Chinese students to educational institutions in the United States to learn about Western technology and military arts. It was hoped that the boys would eventually attend such venerated military institutions as West Point and the Naval Academy, but before they would be eligible for college-level study, the boys had to attend prep schools.

The Phillips Exeter Academy baseball team, including one of the boys from the Chinese Educational Mission in 1881. *Courtesy of Phillips Exeter Academy.*

Led by Yung Wing, who had studied in the United States, the program was headquartered in Connecticut. The boys were the brightest students in China. Schooled for a time in Shanghai to acquire enough skills in English, the first group of thirty boys set sail for the United States in late 1872. They attended many of New England's finest prep schools, and in 1879, five boys arrived in Exeter. Two more would come the next year.

The boys boarded in local homes, the largest number staying with retired minister Jacob Chapman at his house on Middle Street. They were required to return to Connecticut several times each year to continue their Chinese studies, but the remainder of their time was spent in Exeter. Even with the preparation they had received in Shanghai, the boys found life in New England to be very different from that of China, an empire traditionally suspicious of all things foreign. They had been instructed to maintain their Chinese identity and habits. Commissioner Woo Tsze Tun, in a letter to the boys in 1880, reminded them that "since your stay here is brief, as compared with the time you have to spend in China, foreign habits should not become so rooted as that you cannot change them." They were not to violate Chinese tradition by cutting off their long braided queues. They were not to become U.S. citizens. They were not to take American brides. They were not to become Christian. And they were not to succumb to "Western" frivolities—especially the playing of sports.

But not all of their time was taken up in study. It was true that they attended to their schoolwork—these were scholarly boys by their very nature—but they also went to baseball games, attended dances and went to church with their host families. Living with a retired minister and attending a school that began each day with prayer, it would have been impossible for them to ignore the importance of the central messages of nineteenth-century Protestant theology—that of redemption, personal responsibility and individual saving grace.

Chang, in her book *The Chinese in America*, noted that "what the Qing government did not recognize until much later was that these American-educated students would be internally transformed." By 1881, it had become apparent that the boys, although doing well academically, were picking up American customs and habits. It was also becoming obvious that the United States government, far from extending goodwill to China by allowing students to attend public schools, was not going to allow any of them to study at West Point. The United States was on the brink of passing the Chinese Exclusion Act, which forbade Chinese immigration into the country. Bad feelings on both sides led to the end of the program. All the boys, regardless of how far they had come in their studies, were recalled to China in 1881.

The *Exeter News-Letter* sadly announced in early August, "It seems that the cause of the action was a report by a dignitary sent to inspect the schools, which stated that the boys were forgetting the customs of their country and becoming rapidly Americanized. No amount of subsequent explanation was able to correct the erroneous impression thus conveyed, and the order to return is preemptory."

The return to China was difficult for most of the boys. They had been promised a full education and had been looking forward to returning to their country as respectable men. Instead, they were treated as failures—boys who had forsaken their great nation. Kin Ta Ting, who attended Phillips Exeter Academy from 1879 to 1881, wrote to Reverend Chapman, "The Chinese consider denationalization a great crime. This is the chief reason for our recall." He was bitter, and it shows in his early letters.

Most of the Chinese Educational Missionary students went on to do well for themselves in China. A few managed to make it back to the United States, but most did not. Those who remained in China were assigned to military positions or further education. Kin Ta Ting was assigned to the Beiyang Medical School and became a medical officer in the Imperial Army. He was killed in action during the 1900 Boxer Rebellion. Of his time in Exeter, he fondly recalled:

> *I think the P.E.A. Professors ought to be proud of their pupils in China when they hear of their good standing in various schools. That shows the good instructions have been given by them. Their names will never be forgotten by us so long as we live. We often talk of them. How we would like to see their faces again in classrooms! We all want very much to be present at the hundredth anniversary of the Academy. It makes us homesick to think of it.*

CHIN LEE'S LAUNDRY

In the postcard collection of the Exeter Historical Society, there are a few depicting the Trade and Carnival Week parade in 1914. Behind the happy throngs of people on Water Street, standing on a lot that is today populated by coffee-sipping patrons of Me & Ollie's bakery, is the laundry shop of Chin Lee, a Chinese immigrant.

Chinese immigrants first came to the United States during the wild days of the California Gold Rush. The men who arrived expected to work for a few years, send the money home and eventually return. But the amount of money that could be made encouraged many to stay indefinitely. The gold fields had been picked pretty clean by the time most Chinese arrived, but Americans tended to pan only lightly, moving on if they didn't strike it rich immediately. The Chinese went back to the forgotten streams and panned them again, working tirelessly for even the tiniest bit of gold dust. They didn't strike it rich, but they made enough to send home. The real money, it turned out, was in the service industry. Food and laundry were two things the American miners needed. Laundry was sometimes sent by ship all the way to China or Hawaii. It soon became apparent that there was a niche to be filled.

The Chinese also worked in heavy labor jobs, building railroads, doing farm labor or deep-sea fishing. But American racism began to shut most of them out of these jobs. The economic panic of the 1870s brought about unwarranted fears that the Chinese—who were prevented from becoming naturalized citizens or intermarrying with whites—were undermining the job market. A strict immigration law called the Chinese Exclusion Act was passed in 1882 forbidding any Chinese from immigrating to the United States. To the fanatics, it still wasn't enough, and a wave of violence against the Chinese who remained here followed. There were riots in many cities in the West.

As the Chinese came east, the laundry business came with them. According to Iris Chang's *The Chinese in America*, "Opening a laundry appealed to many immigrants because it was a fast way to establish one's own business. It required almost no start-up capital—just a scrub board, soap, and an iron—and operating costs were low since the laundry owner usually saved rent by living in his shop."

By 1900, almost every town in New England had a Chinese laundry. It was a solitary life for the laundryman because he was not allowed to bring his wife or children from China. Denied citizenship, they could not vote. Employers wouldn't hire a worker who was Chinese, and without any employment protections, it was perfectly legal.

The first Chinese laundry in Exeter opened in 1888 and was operated by a man named Sam Song. He sold the business to Chin Han sometime before 1893. The *Exeter News-Letter* noted in March of that year that "Chin Han, a local laundryman, has left Exeter this week for a visit to China." He visited again in 1898 but worried that his reentry into the country would be difficult; he had his picture taken for his passport, an uncommon action at that time. The *News-Letter* noted that the photo was taken by Exeter photographer Newall Nealey.

Han sold the laundry to Charlie Thying in 1910. There is no direct evidence that Mr. Thying was Chinese, but the newspaper published a rather unusual item, noting that "Mr. Thying is a well appearing person and an experienced laundryman. Any boys or persons ill treating or imposing upon him will be prosecuted by Mr. John Scammon." On maps of the town, the shop was still labeled "Chinese Laundry."

Chin Lee bought the business from Charlie Thying. There were never two Chinese laundries in town, although there were other places to get laundry washed. Many people preferred the Chinese hand laundry system, which used no machinery and was easier on the clothes.

When the 1920 census was taken, Chin Lee told the census taker that he had arrived in 1882, making him one of the last Chinese immigrants to come to America legally. He was then fifty-seven years old and married. He lived alone in his rented shop and spoke, but could not write, English. His was a grueling job. "The work consumed almost every waking moment," wrote Iris Chang, "Breathing steam and lint, the laundryman labored on a wet, slippery floor, washing and pressing, using an eight-pound iron heated over a coal stove, and then folding his customers' clothes by hand."

The work eventually took its toll. Chin Lee died in his shop in 1925. A customer found him one morning lying on the floor. The town notified the Chinese Society in Boston, which dispatched his brother and several friends to Exeter to claim his body. Like most Chinese, he was buried temporarily until arrangements could be made to ship his remains home to China, where we believe his gravestone should read, "Chin Lee—a respected laundryman of Exeter, New Hampshire."

THE ARRIVAL OF FRENCH CANADIANS

In 1891, the *Exeter News-Letter* took note of the rising immigrant population in town:

> *What a cosmopolitan population Exeter is acquiring, to be sure. Our Italian residents are rapidly growing in numbers. Then we have our Polish colony of upwards of fifty souls, and rapidly increasing. Our quota of French Canadians is considerably larger than the Poles, and then we have our earlier accessions of English and Irish, the latter counting well into the hundreds. Smaller representations are here from Scotland, France, Germany, Russia, Bulgaria, China and other countries.*

The editor, John Templeton, was an immigrant himself, having arrived at the age of ten from Scotland with his family.

Exeter's original European population had come from England in the 1600s, and the town remained primarily English for its first two hundred

Eno's brickyard on outer Front Street in Exeter. Eno's water-struck bricks were highly prized by Phillips Exeter Academy, which used them for many building projects. When Eno's closed down in 1966, the academy purchased all the remaining back stock.

years. Exeter—actually, New Hampshire in general—considered itself to be a Protestant and English outpost. The New Hampshire Constitution affirmed this by mandating that elected state representatives had to be Protestant, an idea that was only repealed in 1877. But in the mid-1800s, New Hampshire was becoming an industrialized state, and this attracted workers from farther ports. Exeter, like the rest of the state, found itself changing as the new population brought different customs to town.

Irish immigrants began trickling into town just after the Civil War, and after that, the slow stream of people from Canada became a sudden flood. Canada found itself in dire economic straits in the late nineteenth century. The short growing season and expanding population produced intense poverty. With traditional large families, both English-speaking Canadians from the Maritime Provinces and French Canadians from Quebec began to see New England's textile mills as a means to improve life. The journey to America was hardly the arduous one traveled by

Europe's immigrants—from Canada, one merely had to take a train to Boston, Manchester or Lewiston. Those arriving from New Brunswick and Prince Edward Island quickly assimilated into Exeter. Speaking English and worshipping in the local churches was simple for this group.

French Canadians had a bit more difficulty moving within Exeter society. Not only was the language difference a challenge, but they were also Roman Catholic to boot. Exeter was founded by Puritans, who soundly rejected anything and everything that had to do with the "Romanish" church. No liturgical calendar was followed in town—there wasn't even a celebration of Christmas, which was thought of as a pagan bacchanalia by most of the town's population. In many parts of New England, French Canadian immigrants banded together to protect their language and religion, creating neighborhoods of "Little Canada." Exeter was too small for this. They had to figure out how to bridge the gap between English and French customs. The new immigrants learned English and sent their children to the public schools.

But religion was nonnegotiable. By the 1880s, when Exeter's French Canadians had begun to arrive in large numbers, there was a fledgling Catholic church in town. It had been established by Irish immigrants, who had arrived a few decades earlier. Mass was, of course, said in Latin, so there was little difficulty for congregants to participate, but it must have been tough when one's home language was French, the local language was English and the church's language was Latin. The immigrants' children quickly adapted to this crazy tower of Babel, but then the usual pattern of immigrants' language skills hasn't changed much over time—the first generation speaks the home language and haltingly learns the local language, while their children comfortably speak both and grandchildren speak only in the local language. Thelma Cote Barlow, in an interview taped by the historical society for the Girl Scouts in 2006, recalled that when she started school at age six in 1921, "I couldn't speak English and we had a lovely neighbor who was a teacher in first grade. She took me to school until November and she told my parents that by September I'd be able to speak English and I'd be fine in school." "And did you?" I asked. "Yes! And I forgot how to speak French as I grew older!"

In 1901, Joas Jette, who ran a laundry in town, attended a French congress in Springfield, Massachusetts. The *Exeter News-Letter* reported that "he was questioned regarding Exeter's French population. He guessed 85 families and 500 people. Since returning to Exeter he has made a careful canvass for Rev. John Canning of the town and Eno's brickyard. He found 114 French families in town and 11 at the brickyard, numbering respectively 574 and 48 persons, a total of 125 families and 622 persons." Exeter's population at the 1900 census was 4,923 people, with 1,006 listed as "foreign born," making French Canadians the largest immigrant group in town.

Exeter today is still filled with people of French Canadian ancestry. Of the six obituaries published in the *Exeter News-Letter* on April 2, 1926, three of them were people who had been born in Quebec Province and found their way to Exeter: "Mr. Louis Ritchie, Exeter's first citizen of French-Canadian birth, was buried in Exeter last Monday, Rev. Daniel J. Cotter performing a committal service after the funeral in Newmarket, where Mr. Ritchie had latterly lived with a son. He came to Exeter about 1870 with the late Louis Novell, and soon anglicized his name from Richard, as did his early follower, Mr. Beaudoin to Boardman. All were held in the highest esteem, as have been others of their compatriots."

IN SEARCH OF LITHUANIANS

"Were there Lithuanians in Exeter?" I'm often asked this question, probably because my name and the Exeter Historical Society just don't seem to match. Surely a New England town like ours should have a less "ethnic"-sounding curator. Fear not! All is well. Although I am, in fact, a transplant to this town, there were Lithuanians here before me who paved the way.

Tracking down Lithuanians seems like it should be easy, but there are a number of bumps along the way. The first problem is that Lithuania, as a country, didn't actually exist for whole decades. Like Poland, the Baltic states of Estonia, Latvia and Lithuania were often absorbed into other kingdoms and nations. The boundary lines were elastic enough that the people within could have a Polish name but be ethnically Lithuanian or Russian—or any mixture of the three. So it's important to set some clear boundaries about Lithuanian immigration patterns to the United States.

There would not have been any immigration before 1861 unless one were a nobleman or wealthy merchant. Lithuania was under the governance of the Russian empire, where the peasants labored as serfs. Serfdom was not the same as slavery in a few critical ways—serfs were not technically "owned" by a master, but they didn't have freedom to travel or move from their land, so the landlord essentially controlled their lives. Women were expected to move to their husband's family, but unless they were drafted into the tsar's army—a commitment of twenty-five years—men stayed put. So, no one was hopping a boat to America unless they lied about their origins. Abolition of serfdom occurred under Tsar Alexander II just a few years before Abraham Lincoln issued the Emancipation Proclamation in this country.

After emancipation, many Lithuanians began to consider emigration. Improved transportation, droughts, famines and repression of the ethnic minorities by the Russian empire made the decision to leave quite attractive. People arriving from Lithuania were listed as "Russian," so any search must begin by looking for Russians. Indeed, a search of Exeter's vital records does not mention Lithuania as a country of origin until 1913. My great-grandmother's passport, issued in 1914, is entirely in Russian. To add insult to injury (at least for Petronella Benitis), her name on the second page includes a Russian patronymic, Simonovna—a derivation of her father's first name, which she would never have used. Good thing she was illiterate. If she heard it read off at either her place of embarkation or Ellis Island, likely she swallowed her thoughts. For our part, the family is glad that those hated Russians included the patronymic, as it is our only clue about the identity of her father, Simon Benitis.

Lithuanians began to arrive in Exeter in the 1880s. The first to arrive were Jewish immigrants, who most likely were feeling tsarist repression much deeper than the Catholic Lithuanians who followed them here twenty or so years later. Zelig London and his family were quickly joined by the Cohens and Golds by 1887. By 1902, there were more people turning up in Exeter's vital records with "Russia" as a country of origin. Once they arrived, they found work in the many factories in town, married and began to have families. Most have names that are traditionally Lithuanian—ending in *as*, *is* or *us*, such as Mazaluskas, Paszukonis, Raziskis and Cilcius. I'm often told that my name looks Greek for this reason. Many other names have a decidedly Polish feel: Debrowska, Kudroski, Vitkoska and others. These names appear in marriage records and birth registrations. But when we try to find out where the Lithuanian population lived in Exeter, our town directories list no such people. By and large, the Lithuanians altered or completely changed their names—sometimes several times. We recently tried to find the Kopesci family for some visitors to the historical society using directories, census listings and vital records, and it took hours just to determine that they arrived in town with the name "Skopackas" but also used "Skapescki" before settling on "Kopesci." Rather unusually, the name was altered to blend in better with the larger Polish population in Exeter and not the overwhelming English bluebloods who ran the town. I guess they needed to keep some bit of pride.

And by the way, names were *not* changed at Ellis Island. For some reason, lots of families have stories that their names were changed there, but it simply didn't happen. There was no mechanism for name changing in the processes that were used at Ellis Island. Names were often changed, but usually it was the immigrants who changed them. They quickly tired of Americans stumbling over what to them was a simple name. Honestly, "Rimkunas" is perfectly phonetic, yet I've heard all variations of it—usually with a *q* inserted somewhere in the middle.

The first two decades of the twentieth century brought a huge influx of immigrants to the United States. The numbers finally began to abate after 1924, when strict immigration quotas were enacted. Lithuanians in Exeter, as elsewhere in New England, stuck together—even forming a Lithuanian Club that served as a mutual assistance society, paying death, sickness and disability benefits to members. Finding your Lithuanian ancestors can be challenging, but it isn't necessarily impossible. Just don't call them Russians. They don't like that.

Night School

In 1907, the Exeter school board reported that of the 1,028 children registered for classes, 194 were born in another country. As with most immigrant children, they assimilated quickly, learning English in school and absorbing their new culture with ease. Their parents, like most immigrant parents, found the transition much more difficult, and there was little in Exeter to help them along.

The great surge in immigration to the United States began in the late 1800s. Exeter had already seen a rise in immigration from Ireland and Quebec earlier in the century, but by 1890, immigrants had begun to

The Polish American Club lines up for a parade. There were, for a time, three Polish clubs in Exeter, including one for women. The Polish Citizens Club encouraged naturalization, and members flocked to the English night school.

arrive in larger numbers from Poland, Lithuania and Germany, attracted by factory jobs at the Exeter Manufacturing Company, Gale Shoe Shop and Exeter Machine Works.

Then, as now, a sizeable immigrant population brought mixed feelings to the local townspeople. Their labor was welcome, but their native customs seemed odd and their ability to speak a different language was somehow threatening. Just who were these new people, and what where they talking about? In a small-town society where everyone knew everyone else's business, a culturally different subgroup seemed almost secretive. The obvious solution was to make sure that everyone spoke the same language.

First-generation immigrants frequently have a hard time learning a new language—as most of us English speakers would if we were suddenly dropped into downtown Tokyo. The linguistic pattern of immigration hasn't changed over the course of U.S. history—parents speak their native language well and English poorly, their children are comfortably bilingual and the grandchildren speak only English.

The 1890s was also the height of the Gilded Age in America—the age when powerful, wealthy industrialists ruled through corruption and machine politics. The Progressive movement grew out of discontent with this system, and the primary solution to the evils of the machine was education. Literate, educated voters would not easily fall prey to corrupt voting schemes. But providing education for adults was difficult. Local school boards refused to pay for adult education, and the average factory laborer found it hard to find the money and time to attend.

In large cities, the Progressives created settlement houses, community centers where laborers could drop in for information regarding citizenship, hygiene and American culture in general. These were financed entirely by private donations. Exeter was too small for any such institution, but the idea of educating working people through philanthropy was very much alive.

The influx of non-English speakers inspired Rosa Akerman of Exeter to open an evening school targeted toward this new population. Akerman, a widowed former teacher, volunteered her time and sought donations from the community. She opened her school in the fall of 1892 in the Red Men's lodge hall in the Merrill Block on Water Street. Her first class consisted of sixteen men and boys, all eager to improve their English. They paid five cents per class, which was a considerable expense to people earning only a few dollars a week. Mrs. Akerman quickly sought out donations from the public.

Her classes were a great success, but after a few terms, public support waned, and there were no longer enough donations to pay for a place to meet. By 1900, Akerman's school had disbanded.

The idea was revived in 1917. This time, the town was willing to oversee the project. The School Report of 1917 read, "The Evening School, formerly managed and taught by public-spirited citizens, was revived this winter by a joint committee of the Woman's Club and the Civic Club." The local school district oversaw the school, but no local appropriations were made to support it. More than eighty-five people signed up to take classes in basic English ("English for Foreigners," as Helen Tufts, one of the instructors, called it), arithmetic, algebra, bookkeeping, stenography, fancy needlework, woodworking, mechanical drawing and sewing. The most popular classes, by far, were those for improving English language skills.

Spurred on by the patriotism of the First World War, the school flourished for a few years. School superintendent Maro Brooks served on the New Hampshire Committee on Americanization, and he convinced the school board to extend the committee's goals to the town. Immigrant organizations, particularly the Polish Citizens Club, encouraged its members to work toward citizenship. But the unfunded nature of the school and the early arrival of the economic depression in the 1920s ended the school's existence. A frustrated Superintendent Brooks sadly noted in his 1920 report, "The State Board of Education charges superintendents and School Boards with the welfare of Americanization. For us in Exeter a community spirit is growing, and it is hoped that by a pooling of all local efforts along this line, we may do our full share."

Immigration fell off in the following decade. Exeter's Evening School dissolved for nearly ten years before transforming into the adult education system we still have today.

PART VII
Crime and Villains

There's never been a lot of crime in Exeter, but when it does occur, it tends toward the personal. In a town where everyone usually knows everyone else's business, punishment often includes elements of public shame. When this time-honored tradition fails, it is assumed that whatever law was broken must have been a poor one, and it is often difficult to determine who are the bad guys and who are not. Here are a few stories of some of our less-than-stellar criminals.

ROBBERY AT THE OLD EXETER BANK

On Monday morning, June 16, 1828, cashier John Rogers unlocked the doors of the Exeter Bank to discover that it had been robbed over the weekend. Exeter author Albertus T. Dudley would later describe the room as "a scene of pillage, the floor littered with blacksmith's tools, the big iron treasure chest gaping empty. Gone were the neat packages of bank bills and the heavy bags of specie; even the historic Spanish doubloon salvaged from the sunken galleon *Assumpcion* by Ebenezer Clifford with his newly invented diving bell had disappeared." Also, $28,000 was missing. There was little evidence to trace, and the burglars were already two days away.

Judge Jeremiah Smith (1759–1842) served as bank director for the Exeter Bank. Not content to let robbers of his bank escape, he pursued the criminals across several states.

Banknotes such as this one were issued by individual banks, making it easier to trace cash if it was stolen.

Finding the robbers was a task left to the bank director, Jeremiah Smith. Smith was no usual bank director. He had served in the New Hampshire legislature and the U.S. House of Representatives. He'd been chief justice of the New Hampshire Supreme Judicial Court not once but twice. He'd also been the state's governor. With no one else to do the job, he became the chief detective in tracking down the robbers.

Exeter was a small town, and local people immediately began to buzz about anything that had seemed unusual in the previous weeks. Two strange men had been seen camping in the woods in the Oaklands. A number of people had encountered the men, and they all described the same features. One man was rather nondescript and wore a black coat and a big hat. The other was a pockmarked Irishman. One witness was Exeter's venerable Dr. William Perry, who couldn't resist a bit of armchair diagnosis when he later testified, "The forward one was much pock broken, and on noticing it, I thought of the severity of that disease which had left its marks so deeply on his face. He gave me a side look and I passed on."

The pockmarked Irishman seemed disinclined to maintain a low profile while in town. The one habit that made him noticed wherever he went was a drinking problem. Instead of bellying up to the bar and ordering cider, ale or rum—like most people—he ordered milk. His milk habit would be his downfall, noticed by everyone who came into contact with him, starting with farmer James Gilman. Gilman noticed that his cow was dry in the mornings. He had no real proof, but the men were seen nearby; he later testified that "in May last one of my cows appeared to have been milked by strangers." The problem went away, he said, when he moved the cows to a different pasture.

Smith quickly determined that men fitting the local description were seen going through the turnpike bridge on the way to Newburyport. In Newburyport, Judge Smith identified the men as Philip Kimball and William Lorne, both originally from Newport, Rhode Island, but currently living in Freetown, Massachusetts. When the men arrived in Freetown, they headed for the home of Malone Briggs, another shady character. Kimball immediately began spending money freely, buying himself a new suit and showing off wads of cash. He, Lorne and Briggs then took a trip to New York to visit Briggs's son, Benjamin. According to Albertus T. Dudley, "Lorne getting off a day later than the others because he had succumbed to the temptation to turn aside for a draft of milk and so missed the boat."

They then returned to Newport and spent freely at a local auction. By this time, people had begun to get suspicious. The local papers had run several stories about the robbery at Exeter, and residents were on the lookout for banknotes from New Hampshire. The men were detained, and Judge Smith hurried down with the bank's cashier. They had no direct evidence connecting the men with the break-in; the only hope was to identify the actual money. Alas, the banknotes confiscated in Newport were common and could not be tied to Exeter. A packet of cash was found in a Newport pigpen near where the men were arrested—this money still had the cashier's wrappings and was clearly some of the stolen money. But it wasn't found on the men.

Smith then traveled to Freetown to talk with a very annoyed Mrs. Briggs. She'd spent her entire married life worrying over her sketchy husband's activities and willingly allowed Smith to search the house. He found nothing inside but was able to locate a handmade key to the Exeter Bank and some cash in a crevice in a stone wall. The remainder of the money, including Ebenezer Clifford's doubloon, was quickly located at disparate places in Freetown, Topsfield and New York near Ben Briggs's store. Judge Smith never revealed how he uncovered the many locations, but most likely he wormed the information out of Malone Briggs, who never faced charges as an accessory.

A trial was held in Keene in September. Even though the prosecutors had no direct evidence, Kimball and the pockmarked, milk-drinking Lorne were convicted and sent to prison. Judge Smith successfully located all but $500 of the stolen funds. He proved to be a man unwilling to take crime lightly.

Exeter's Liquor Raids

In 1888, New Hampshire elected David Harvey Goodell as governor. A Republican from Antrim, Goodell was an inventor and businessman who was probably best known for his work with the temperance movement. As president of the Anti-Saloon League, he felt that the long-neglected liquor laws in New Hampshire needed to be enforced

The Granite House Hotel stood on Center Street in Exeter. It was the site of numerous liquor raids.

vigorously. A spate of alcohol-related crimes had brought the issue to the forefront by 1890, and in December of that year, Goodell issued a proclamation:

> *In view of the various heinous crimes which have been committed in our State within the past few weeks, directly traceable to the use of intoxicating liquors, in the sale of which the criminal laws of the State have been flagrantly violated: Now therefore, I do hereby warn all persons engaged in this illegal and deadly traffic to desist there from immediately, and I call upon the Attorney General of the State, the Solicitors and Sheriffs of the counties, the Mayors of the cities and the Selectmen of the towns, and all other officers of the law throughout the State, and upon all good citizens of every party, sect and faith to unite in one supreme effort to close up and suppress every liquor saloon of every description within our borders.*

In Exeter, there were any number of saloons and places where one could get a drink with minimal regulation. The town selectmen rarely enforced liquor laws, and although it was illegal for any unlicensed establishment to sell alcohol, the police were rarely called out on violations. Drunkenness was a problem—town meetings were frequently

Ned Shute, although not mentioned in the text, was the primary enforcer of the liquor laws in town. As the laws had been ignored for years, most citizens, although opposed to public drunkenness, also took umbrage with the heavy fines imposed on local businessmen.

interrupted by the intoxicated ramblings of the one or two known town drunkards, and there was a great deal of concern about students being served alcohol without any restrictions.

A letter from "A Citizen" published in the *Exeter News-Letter* shortly after Goodell's proclamation supported the governor's position: "The need of the law's enforcement in Exeter is certainly apparent. Never was the saloon a more prominent factor than at present. Never was intemperance producing its harvest under more favorable conditions. The deadly traffic is increasing without let or hindrance. Its painful effects are more and more manifest every day. We may well enquire: What shall the end be?"

The *News-Letter* issued the following warning: "The selectmen have notified all saloon keepers that prompt and vigorous prosecution will follow in all cases where sales are known to have been made to minors, students, habitual drunkards or intoxicated persons, and sales on Sunday will be likewise treated. In this move the officials will have the support of all classes."

All of the local restaurants and inns were subject to police raids. In turn, the Granite House, Phoenix House, Quincy House and even some of the licensed saloons, such as those of George Pease and Andrew McGlincey, were cited for liquor violations. Fines were stiff—often as much as $200—but most of the proprietors seemed to feel that a profit could still be made. One raid would often follow another, with fines paid and liquor stocks seized.

The problem of what to do with all that seized liquor was another issue altogether. If the saloon were licensed, the liquor still belonged to the owner but could not be sold in town after the raid. Fred Upton pleaded guilty to illegal sales, and according to the *News-Letter*, "His stock of liquors has been returned to him, and shipped out of state." But if the town took possession of the illegal stock, authorities had to figure out what to do with it. In September 1891, after a particularly successful raid, the liquor was brought to the police lockup. The *News-Letter* reported the following week that the liquor

was placed by the police authorities in a cell of the lockup, of which the door was securely locked. Sunday night the lockup had seven occupants, who contrived by means of a broom inserted between the bars of the door to overturn a barrel of liquor, in such a manner that the spigot end fell next to the door. To crush in the sides of a tin dipper so that it would pass between two bars was an easy matter, and the thirsty prisoners soon drank themselves into a condition of thorough stupor. Later in the week two tramps made away with the contents of a demi-john overlooked when the stock was removed from the cell.

The following year, the problem was solved. "Much of the stock of liquors confiscated in recent raids by the local police has been delivered to the county solicitor, by whom it has been forwarded to the county farm for medicinal use."

Gradually, it was determined that raiding the local businesses wasn't stopping the problem of public intoxication. By 1893, the *News-Letter* grimly commented, "Liquor raids having at last become fruitless of results, attention has now been directed against the owners of buildings leased for saloon purposes."

In 1895, the town established a liquor agency to sell alcohol for medicinal, mechanical and chemical purposes. By 1910, the town had voted itself dry, and spirituous liquors disappeared until the repeal of national prohibition in 1933.

THE IRON HALL

There was no place called the Iron Hall in Exeter—in fact, there was no Iron Hall anywhere. The Order of the Iron Hall was an organization founded in Indianapolis, Indiana, in 1881 that spawned branches all over the United States until it became insolvent and disbanded in scandal in 1892.

Fraternal organizations and friendly societies flourished in the latter half of the nineteenth century. In a time before adequate insurance coverage or government safeguards, many joined these organizations to take advantage of the benefits they paid out. Membership fees and annual dues were invested, and members received a guaranteed payment in the event of sickness or death. There was also a strong social element to these clubs, and they tended to attract men from particular occupations or ethnic backgrounds.

Most fraternal groups created secret rituals and elaborate initiation rites. Although they considered themselves to be "secret" societies, they weren't entirely secret. The Improved Order of Red Men in Exeter proudly marched in parades—in full Indian regalia—in the early part of the twentieth century.

Exeter's 1901 directory lists eleven such organizations, including the Masons, the Improved Order of Odd Fellows, the Knights of Pythias, the Good Templars, the Improved Order of Red Med, the Ancient Order of Workmen, the Foresters of America and the Royal Arcanum. There were also clubs for Exeter's Polish and Lithuanian communities. All of these groups combined fellowship and mutual assistance. It was also possible to join as many groups as one liked, and it wasn't uncommon to read, in a man's obituary, that he'd belonged to as many as three or four different organizations. Attending meetings could keep him busy every night of the week—not such a bad thing in the days before television and PTA meetings. Expenses were minimal, and the group supplied both a group identity and financial support in hard times.

With so many groups forming, it was no surprise when, in 1888, yet another organizer appeared in town eager to sign up members. The Supreme Justice F.D. Somerby arrived in town in March to enroll members in the Order of the Iron Hall. Numbers are hard to find for a secret society, but the *Exeter News-Letter* noted that by October of that year, "twenty-nine members joined the local branch of the Iron Hall Monday evening." Oddly, or in retrospect suspiciously, none of the recruiting articles mentioned what the Iron Hall's goals were.

Somerby, Iron Hall's founder and chief spokesman, held a meeting at Exeter's opera house the following March to explain the group's aims, and it was something of a surprise to many. The Iron Hall was sold to the public as a fraternal organization, and as such, it provided small payments to members for sickness, but it had none of the usual death benefits. Instead, it functioned as an investment club. Each member would pay $300 into the group and within seven years would receive $1,000—an amazing return on such an investment. It sounded unlikely, but the smooth-talking Somerby calmed any concerns. The *News-Letter* even commented, "His illustration of the practical working of cooperation was most amusing and effective. Mr. Somerby is a pleasing speaker who is thoroughly at home with his subject and believes fully in its merits." He even held up a handful of certificates made out to members in Cambridge, Massachusetts.

Enthusiasm to join was encouraging. After the opera house meeting, the *News-Letter* reported that "a new branch of the Iron Hall is being formed in town, and special inducements are offered to persons joining before the charter is closed. Already some of the leading men of Exeter both in professional and business life have handed in their names to the organizer of the branch, and a cordial invitation is extended to all the citizens of Exeter and vicinity to unite with the order."

But there is nothing that can return at the rates the Iron Hall promised. Somerby's financial structure was a classic pyramid scheme based on recruiting new members. The scheme also depended on some members lapsing on their payments or dying before the seven-year period ended. But the faulty accounting caught up with the group, and it was placed in receivership.

Munsey's Magazine published an article in its 1892 edition that called the Iron Hall "The Wonderful Career of a Delusion." After discussing at length the faulty accounting of the organization, the editor summed up, "As the properly rounded out sermon is supposed to end with its text, we may conclude by repeating that it is strange, in these days when ciphering is taught in all the common schools, that a 'two dollars for a dollar' concern should find a hundred thousand contributors."

The last time Iron Hall was mentioned in Exeter was in 1896, when it was noted that the New Hampshire State branch arrived in town and was "in consultation with local members of the order." No doubt it was attempting to figure the losses. As the old saying goes, if it looks too good to be true, it probably is.

THE KINGSTON STOWAWAYS

In June 1896, Albert and Lucy Tyler set out from Exeter for a trip west. The two had been married just over two years earlier and must have been looking for a bit of adventure. The trip would not turn out exactly as expected, although it definitely did become an "adventure" and they would justly earn their fifteen minutes of fame.

The trip appears to have begun as a pleasure excursion. The *Exeter Gazette*, a rival of the *Exeter News-Letter*, noted that they set out from Kingston "in a pneumatic run-about wagon, drawn by a horse, Peter. At Des Moines, Iowa, they purchased another horse and then made the rest of the trip to the Pacific with two horses. They were nine days

A lightweight "run-about" carriage, such as this one owned by Dr. William Perry, was useful for quick trips. It was designed for speed rather than heavy travel. The Tylers would discover that it was not a particularly good vehicle for a cross-country trip.

on the Great American desert, and arrived at Los Angelos [*sic*], Cal., after being on the road just 180 days." A "run-about" was a small, lightweight carriage. It was the favored type of transportation for doctors and fire chiefs because it could be pulled by a single horse and hitched up quickly. With air-filled tires, it was well suited to town and city roads that were well maintained. But it was hardly the type of transportation one might take on a long, arduous, cross-country trip. It had neither fenders nor heavy tops to weigh it down and little space for luggage.

The two lingered in California for a while before heading to Seattle. It may have been the lure of gold that brought them north. Gold had been discovered in Alaska and the Yukon River Basin in Canada while the Tylers were making their trip, and 1897 would prove to be the summer of the Klondike Gold Rush.

Albert and Lucy were nearly there, but their finances had mostly run out. Albert had tried to support them by "trade"—perhaps dealing in merchandise as his father, Rolla Tyler, of Exeter, did back home—but it wasn't enough. The *Gazette* reported that the couple found themselves "living in a tent near the corner of Second Avenue and Virginia Street." At this point, they decided that they had to get out of Seattle one way or another and hatched a plan to get out. Mr. Tyler would later tell a railroad official that "little obstacles to a pleasure trip across the country like those they had just encountered, did not discourage them, and that sooner or later they would go out of Seattle." And so, they determined to head back east to Boston.

"Being without funds," the *Gazette* continued, "they hit upon the scheme of getting a piano box and fitting it out for a transcontinental trip to the bean-eating town." An upright piano box would have been three feet deep, five feet tall and six feet long. Not roomy by any stretch of the imagination, but they weren't planning to spend too much time actually in the box. "One side of the box was fixed so that the boards could be removed and thus allow exit. The plan was to open up the box, once on the road, and then enjoy the freedom of the car," noted the *Gazette*.

Unfortunately, once they had packed themselves inside, the freight wagon delivered them to the rail station fifteen minutes after the train left. The box was moved to storage, where someone began to hear noises from within. Opening the top, a woman's voice piped up and said, "Hello!" "Freight Agent Allen could hardly believe his ears. He looked down into the box and discovered that the salutation came from a little woman clad only in her night gown. Further inspection revealed also a man clad in abbreviated costume. The remainder of the box was taken up with a supply of provisions, including apples, crackers, figs, bread, onions and water. The human freight was not shipped."

Because they hadn't actually been taken on the train, Albert and Lucy hadn't broken any laws. Albert produced his marriage certificate as proof of their identity, and they were apparently free to go. They called an express wagon and packed up their supplies, and "as they went away from the station the man waved his hand derisively toward the railroad people saying: 'Ta, ta, I'll see you in the Klondyke!'"—perhaps to throw them off his track.

But the railroad got its revenge on Albert and Lucy, releasing the story to the newspapers. It hit the wires and was picked up by the *Boston Journal*, which quickly relayed the story to Exeter. When the couple finally arrived in Exeter a few weeks later—by train, no less—they were embarrassed to find themselves a media sensation. The *Gazette* caught up with them and asked about the incident. "This story they both deny, and say that the parties who made the attempt, were caught and gave their names, thus making it appear as if it was Mr. and Mrs. Tyler, when in fact, it was not." But the *News-Letter* gave them no such denial, stating only, "Mr. and Mrs. Albert Tyler, whose attempt to ship themselves east from Seattle, Wash., in a piano box, was a recent sensation, are now at Mrs. Tyler's old home in Kingston." And with that, their brush with fame ended.

About the Author

Barbara Rimkunas has been the curator at the Exeter Historical Society since 2000. She is the author of *Exeter: Historically Speaking*, published in 2008 by The History Press. She writes a biweekly column, "Historically Speaking," for the *Exeter News-Letter*.

She began her career in history as a student field researcher for the University of Maine's archaeology department. She later taught high school in Portland, Maine, and Newmarket, New Hampshire. She has been a member of the Girl Scouts of USA since 1970 and is currently a troop leader in Exeter. She is an avid reader, knitter and bicyclist and does not collect gnomes. She lives in Exeter, New Hampshire, with her husband, Mike Nickerson, and daughters—all of whom rarely read her newspaper columns but justify this by (correctly) arguing that after listening to her discuss a given topic for weeks on end, they've had enough.